FM 3-13

INFORMATION
OPERATIONS

D1806044

DECEMBER 2016

DISTRIBUTION RESTRICTION:

Approved for public release; distribution is unlimited

HEADQUARTERS, DEPARTMENT OF THE ARMY

SUPERCESSION STATEMENT: This publication supersedes FM 3-13, 25 Jan 2013.

Other books we publish on Amazon.com

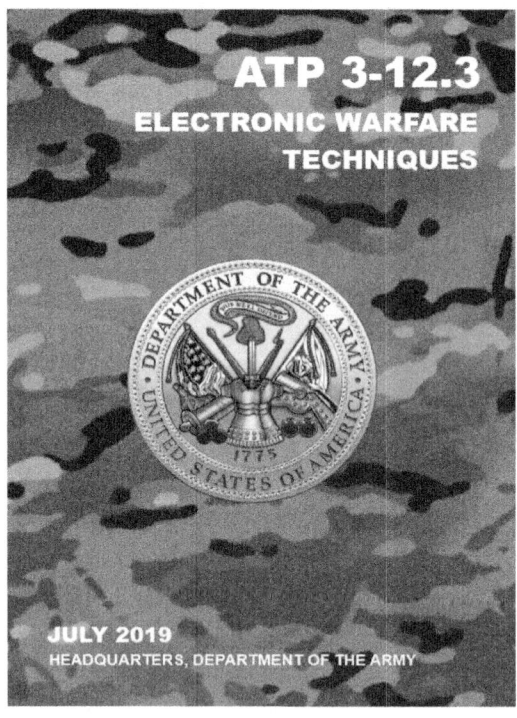

Field Manual
No. 3-13

Headquarters
Department of the Army
Washington, DC, 6 December 2016

Information Operations

Contents

Distribution Restriction: Approved for public release; distribution is unlimited.

*This publication supersedes FM 3-13, 25 January 2013.

Figures

Tables

Preface

Field Manual (FM) 3-13, *Information Operations*, serves as the Army's foundational doctrine for information operations. The purpose of this edition is to better align Army doctrine with joint doctrine, while recognizing the unique requirements of information operations in support of the land force. FM 3-13 discusses the conduct of information operations in today's complex global security environment, which requires a dynamic range of capabilities and skills: from technological capabilities, such as cyberspace operations; to individual capabilities, such as speaking a foreign language; from technical skills, such as those required to defend computer networks; to interpersonal skills, such as those required to conduct Soldier and leader engagements. This manual provides overarching guidance to effectively integrate information operations into the operations process in order to create decisive effects in the information environment.

The principal audience for FM 3-13 is all members of the Profession of Arms. Commanders and staffs of Army headquarters serving as joint task force or multinational headquarters should also refer to applicable joint or multinational doctrine concerning the range of military operations and joint or multinational forces. Trainers and educators throughout the Army will also use this manual.

Commanders, staffs, and subordinates ensure their decisions and actions comply with applicable United States, international, and, in some cases, host-nation laws and regulations. Commanders at all levels ensure their Soldiers operate in accordance with the law of war and the rules of engagement. (See Field Manual 27-10.)

FM 3-13 uses joint terms where applicable. Selected joint and Army terms and definitions appear in both the glossary and the text. Terms for which FM 3-13 is the proponent publication (the authority) are italicized in the text and are marked with an asterisk (*) in the glossary. Terms and definitions for which FM 3-13 is the proponent publication are boldfaced in the text. For other definitions shown in the text, the term is italicized and the number of the proponent publication follows the definition.

This manual seeks to minimize the use of acronyms but will use two acronyms routinely: IO for information operations and IRC for information-related capability. If other acronyms are employed, their use will be limited to the paragraph or section in which they appear, or a legend will be available.

FM 3-13 applies to the Active Army, Army National Guard (ARNG)/Army National Guard of the United States (ARNGUS), and the United States Army Reserve (USAR) unless otherwise stated.

The proponent for this publication is the U.S. Combined Arms Center, Information Operations Proponent Office. The preparing agency is the Combined Arms Doctrine Directorate, United States Army Combined Arms Center. Send written comments and recommendations on a Department of the Army (DA) Form 2028 (Recommended Changes to Publications and Blank Forms) directly to Commander, United States Army Combined Arms Center and Fort Leavenworth, ATTN: ATZL-MCK-D (FM 3-13), 300 McPherson Avenue, Fort Leavenworth, KS 66027-2337; by e-mail to: usarmy.leavenworth.mccoe.mbx.cadd-org-mailbox@mail.mil; or submit an electronic DA Form 2028.

ACKNOWLEDGMENTS

Assessing and Evaluating Department of Defense Efforts to Inform, Influence, and Persuade: Desk Reference. Copyright © 2015. Christopher Paul, Jessica Yeats, Colin P. Clarke, & Miriam Matthews. RAND National Defense Research Institute.

Assessing and Evaluating Department of Defense Efforts to Inform, Influence, and Persuade: Handbook for Practitioners. Copyright © 2015. Christopher Paul, Jessica Yeats, Colin P. Clarke, & Miriam Matthews. RAND National Defense Research Institute.

Assessing and Evaluating Department of Defense Efforts to Inform, Influence, and Persuade: An Annotated Reading List. Copyright © 2015. Christopher Paul, Jessica Yeats, Colin P. Clarke, & Miriam Matthews. RAND National Defense Research Institute.

Dominating Duffer's Domain: Lessons for the 21st-Century Information Operations Practitioner (Report written for the Marine Corps Information Operations Center) Copyright © 2015. Christopher Paul and William Marcellino. RAND National Defense Research Institute.

Introduction

Over the past two decades, Army information operations (IO) has gone through a number of doctrinal evolutions, explained, in part, by the rapidly changing nature of information, its flow, processing, dissemination, impact and, in particular, its military employment. At the same time, a decade and a half of persistent conflict and global engagement have taught us a lot about the nature of the information environment, especially that in any given area of operations, this environment runs the gamut from the most technologically-advanced to the least. Army units employ IO to create effects in and through the information environment that provide commanders a decisive advantage over adversaries, threats, and enemies in order to defeat the opponent's will. Simultaneously, Army units engage with and influence other relevant foreign audiences to gain their support for friendly objectives. Commanders' IO contributes directly to tactical and operational success and supports objectives at the strategic level.

This latest version of FM 3-13 returns to the joint definition of IO, although it clarifies that land forces must do more than affect threat decision making if they are to accomplish their mission. They must also protect their own decision making and the information that feeds it; align their actions, messages and images; and engage and influence relevant targets and audiences in the area of operations. While the term *inform and influence activities* has been rescinded, many of the principles espoused in the last version of FM 3-13 carry forward, especially the synchronization of information-related capabilities (IRCs).

IRCs are those capabilities that generate effects in and through the information environment, but these effects are almost always accomplished in combination with other information-related capabilities. Only through their effective synchronization can commanders gain a decisive advantage over adversaries, threats, and enemies in the information environment. While capabilities such as military information support operations, combat camera, military deception, operations security and cyberspace operations are readily considered information-related, commanders consider any capability an IRC that is employed to create effects and operationally-desirable conditions within a dimension of the information environment.

FM 3-13 contains nine chapters:

Chapter 1 provides an overview of information operations. This overview includes an understanding of the operational and information environments; the definition of IO and the definition's component parts; IO's purpose; and how IO contributes to combat power.

Chapter 2 discusses how IO supports decisive action through three weighted efforts: attack, defend, and stabilize. It also discusses three enabling activities that units must perform to ensure IO supports decisive action effectively.

Chapter 3 overviews the roles, responsibilities, relationships, and organizations that lead, plan, support, and conduct IO. It involves the commander down to the individual Soldier.

Chapters 4-7 examine IO's integration into the operations process. Chapter 4 discusses Planning; Chapter 5, Preparation; Chapter 6, Execution; and Chapter 7, Targeting Integration.

Chapter 8 examines the assessment of IO. While IO does not employ a separate assessment methodology, it does have unique considerations for which units must account.

Chapter 9 discusses IO at brigade and below. It provides insights for units to consider when planning, preparing, executing, and assessing IO at these levels.

Chapter 1

Information Operations Overview

1-1.   Conflict is fundamentally a contest of wills. Winning this contest requires commanders to employ combat power to execute decisive action across the range of military operations. *Combat power* is the total means of destructive, constructive, and information capabilities that a military unit or formation can apply at a given time (ADRP 3-0). Combat power is comprised of eight elements, the last six of which are warfighting functions: leadership, information, mission command, movement and maneuver, intelligence, fires, sustainment, and protection.

1-2.   Information operations (IO) creates effects in and through the information environment. IO optimizes the information element of combat power and supports and enhances all other elements in order to gain an operational advantage over an enemy or adversary. These effects are intended to influence, disrupt, corrupt or usurp enemy or adversary decision making and everything that enables it, while enabling and protecting friendly decision making. Because IO's central focus is affecting decision making and, by extension, the will to fight, commanders personally ensure IO is integrated into operations from the start.

SECTION I –OPERATIONAL AND INFORMATION ENVIRONMENTS

1-3.   An *operational environment* is a composite of the conditions, circumstances, and influences that affect the employment of capabilities and bear on the decisions of the commander (JP 3-0). It encompasses physical areas and factors of the air, land, maritime, space, and cyberspace domains, and the information environment, which includes cyberspace. The *information environment* is the aggregate of individuals, organizations, and systems that collect, process, disseminate, or act on information (JP 3-13). Although an operational environment and information environment are defined separately, they are interdependent and integral to the other.

OPERATIONAL ENVIRONMENT

1-4.   Several characteristics of the operational environment have a significant impact on land force operations. Each of these characteristics has a significant information aspect. They are:
- Speed and diffusion of information.
- Information asymmetry.
- Proliferation of cyberspace and space capabilities.
- Operations among populations.

1-5.   Across the globe, information is increasingly available in near-real time. The ability to access this information, from anywhere, at any time, broadens and accelerates human interaction, across multiple levels (person to person, person to organization, person to government, government to government). Social media, in particular, enables the swift mobilization of people and resources around ideas and causes, even before they are fully understood. Disinformation and propaganda create malign narratives that can propagate quickly and instill an array of emotions and behaviors from anarchy to focused violence. From a military standpoint, information enables decision making, leadership, and combat power; it is also critical to seizing, gaining and retaining the initiative, and consolidating gains in the operational environment.

1-6.   Threats, large and small, increasingly operate in an indeterminate zone between peace and war. They seek to avoid U.S. strengths and, instead take advantage of U.S. laws and policies regarding the use of information and cyber capabilities. Coupled with the nation's initial reluctance to engage in major combat operations, they achieve incremental gains that advance their agenda and narrative. They use a range of techniques including non-attribution, innuendo, propaganda, disinformation, and misinformation to sway global opinion favorable to their aims.

1-7. States and non-states are rapidly expanding their investment in cyberspace and space capabilities and forces. They recognize the leveling effect these domains, especially cyberspace, offer in terms of achieving parity or overmatch at minimum relative cost. A significant portion of the threat's information asymmetry comes from its growing capacity in space and cyberspace.

1-8. Threats operate among populations with whom they often share cultural or ethnic identity, making it difficult to distinguish threat from non-threat. This fact requires U.S. forces to interact and communicate, in nuanced fashion, with a wide range of audiences and actors in order to separate those willing to support U.S. intentions from those who are not. The ability of the threat to operate among populations and harness commonalities provides the threat yet another asymmetric advantage.

INFORMATION ENVIRONMENT

1-9. The information environment is not separate or distinct from the operational environment but inextricably part of it. In fact, any activity that occurs in the information environment simultaneously occurs in and affects one or more of the operational environment domains.

1-10. The information environment is comprised of three dimensions: physical, informational, and cognitive. Within the physical dimension of the information environment is the connective infrastructure that supports the transmission, reception, and storage of information. Also within this dimension are tangible actions or events that transmit a message in and of themselves, such as patrols, aerial reconnaissance, and civil affairs projects. Within the informational dimension is the content or data itself. The informational dimension refers to content and flow of information, such as text or images, or data that staffs can collect, process, store, disseminate, and display. The informational dimension provides the necessary link between the physical and cognitive dimensions. Within the cognitive dimension are the minds of those who are affected by and act upon information. These minds range from friendly commanders and leaders, to foreign audiences affecting or being affected by operations, to enemy, threat or adversarial decision makers. This dimension focuses on the societal, cultural, religious, and historical contexts that influence the perceptions of those producing the information and of the targets and audiences receiving the information. In this dimension, decision makers and target audiences are most prone to influence and perception management.

1-11. The information environment has increased in complexity. Due to the widespread availability of the Internet, wireless communications and information, the information environment has become an even more important consideration to military planning and operations, because the military increasingly relies on these technologies. Activities occurring in and through the information environment have a consequential effect on the operational environment and can impact military operations and outcomes. Therefore, commanders and their staffs must understand the information environment, in all its complexity, and the potential impacts it will have on current and planned military operations.

SECTION II – INFORMATION OPERATIONS DEFINED AND DESCRIBED

1-12. *Information Operations* (IO) is the integrated employment, during military operations, of information-related capabilities in concert with other lines of operation to influence, disrupt, corrupt, or usurp the decision-making of adversaries and potential adversaries while protecting our own (JP 3-13). This manual uses the term IO comprehensively to capture all activity employed to affect the information environment and contribute to operations in and through the information environment. IO includes:

- Integration and synchronization of information-related capabilities.
- Planning, preparing, execution, and assessment.
- The capability and capacity that ensures the accomplishment of IO, to include the units and personnel responsible for its conduct.

Breaking down the definition into constituent parts helps to understand its meaning and implications for land forces.

INTEGRATED EMPLOYMENT OF INFORMATION-RELATED CAPABILITIES (IRCS)

1-13. IO brings together IRCs at a specific time and in a coherent fashion to create effects in and through the information environment that advance the ability to deliver operational advantage to the commander. While IRCs create individual effects, IO stresses aggregate and synchronized effects as essential to achieving operational objectives.

1-14. An *information-related capability* (IRC) is a tool, technique, or activity employed within a dimension of the information environment that can be used to create effects and operationally desirable conditions (JP 1-02). The formal definition of IRCs encourages commanders and staffs to employ all available resources when seeking to affect the information environment to operational advantage. For example, if artillery fires are employed to destroy communications infrastructure that enables enemy decision making, then artillery is an IRC in this instance. In daily practice, however, the term IRC tends to refer to those tools, techniques, or activities that are inherently information-based or primarily focused on affecting the information environment. These include—

- Military deception.
- Military information support operations (MISO).
- Soldier and leader engagement (SLE), to include police engagement.
- Civil affairs operations.
- Combat camera.
- Operations security (OPSEC).
- Public affairs.
- Cyberspace electromagnetic activities.
- Electronic warfare.
- Cyberspace operations.
- Space operations.
- Special technical operations.

1-15. All unit operations, activities, and actions affect the information environment. Even if they primarily affect the physical dimension, they nonetheless also affect the informational and cognitive dimensions. For this reason, whether or not they are routinely considered an IRC, a wide variety of unit functions and activities can be adapted for the purposes of conducting information operations or serve as enablers to its planning, execution, and assessment. Some of these include, but are not limited to:

- Commander's communications strategy or communication synchronization.
- Presence, profile, and posture.
- Foreign disclosure.
- Physical security.
- Physical maneuver.
- Special access programs.
- Civil military operations.
- Intelligence.
- Destruction and lethal actions.

DURING MILITARY OPERATIONS

1-16. Army forces, as part of a joint force, conduct operations across the conflict continuum and range of military operations. Whether participating in security cooperation efforts or conducting major combat operations, IO is essential during all phases (0 through V) of a military operation. (See JP 5-0 for a detailed discussion of the joint phasing model).

IN CONCERT WITH OTHER LINES OF OPERATION

1-17. Commanders use lines of operations and lines of effort to visualize and describe operations. A *line of operations* is a line that defines the directional orientation of a force in time and space in relation to the enemy and that links the force with its base of operations and objectives (ADRP 3-0). Lines of operations connect a series of decisive points that lead to control of a geographic or force-oriented objective. A *line of effort* is a line that links multiple tasks using the logic of purpose rather than geographical reference to focus efforts toward establishing operational and strategic conditions (ADRP 3-0). Lines of effort are essential to long-term planning when positional references to an enemy or adversary have little relevance. Commanders may describe an operation along lines of operations, lines of effort, or a combination of both. Commanders, supported by their staff, ensure information operations are integrated into the concept of operation to support each line of operation and effort. Based on the situation, commanders may designate IO as a line of effort to synchronize actions and focus the force on creating desired effects in the information environment. Depending on the type of operation or the phase, commanders may designate an IO-focused line of effort as decisive.

TO INFLUENCE, DISRUPT, CORRUPT, OR USURP

1-18. IO seeks to create specific effects at a specific time and place. Predominantly, these effects occur in and through the information environment. Immediate effects (disrupt, corrupt, usurp) are possible in the information environment's physical and informational dimensions through the denial, degradation, or destruction of adversarial or enemy information-related capabilities. However, effects in the cognitive dimension (influence) take longer to manifest. It is these cognitive effects—as witnessed through changed behavior—that matter most to achieving decisive outcomes.

THE DECISION MAKING OF ENEMIES AND ADVERSARIES

1-19. While there are differences among the terms adversaries, threats, and enemies, all three refer to those individuals, organizations, or entities that oppose U.S. efforts. They therefore must be influenced in some fashion to acquiesce or surrender to or otherwise support U.S. national objectives by aligning their actions in concert with commanders' intent. [The joint phrasing "adversaries and potential adversaries" is revised to "enemies and adversaries" to better align with Army terminology.]

1-20. Affecting enemy and adversary decision making necessitates affecting all contributing factors that enable it. These factors include, but are not limited to:
- Command and control systems, as well as other systems that facilitate decision making.
- Communications systems.
- Information content (words, images, symbols).
- Staffs, advisors, counselors, and confidants.
- Human networks and constituencies that influence the decision maker and to whom the decision maker seeks to influence; in other words, all relevant audiences in the areas of operations and interest.

WHILE PROTECTING OUR OWN

1-21. Friendly commanders, like enemy and adversary leaders, depend on an array of systems, capabilities, information, networks, and decision aids to assist in their decision making. Gaining operational advantage in the information environment is equally about exploiting and protecting the systems, information, and people that speed and enhance friendly decision making, as it is about denying the same to the threat.

THE PURPOSE OF INFORMATION OPERATIONS

1-22. The purpose of IO is to create effects in and through the information environment that provide commanders decisive advantage over enemies and adversaries. Commanders achieve this advantage in several ways: preserve and facilitate decision making and the impact of decision making, while influencing, disrupting or degrading enemy or adversary decision making; get required information faster and with greater accuracy and clarity than the enemy or adversary; or influence the attitudes and behaviors of relevant audiences in the area of operations having an impact on operations and decision making.

1-23. To support achievement of these various ways, IO employs and synchronizes IRCs to affect the will, awareness, understanding, and capability of these audiences, while protecting our own. Will, awareness, understanding, and capability all contribute to and sustain decision making and, if compromised, can impair that decision making. In terms of will, awareness, understanding, and capability, advantage is achieved when commanders preserve their will to fight, as well as their situational understanding and their full capacity and ability to prosecute operations. Further, commanders achieve advantage when they preserve their freedom of action in the information environment while degrading enemy or adversary freedom of action.

THREE INTERRELATED EFFORTS

1-24. IO is comprised of three inter-related efforts: a commander-led staff planning and synchronization effort; a preparation and execution effort carried out by IRC units, IO units, or staff entities in concert with the IO working group; and an assessment effort carried out by all involved. These three efforts work in tandem and overlap each other.

1-25. The planning and synchronization effort includes planning and synchronizing IRC employment to create effects in and through the information environment that result in advantage over the threat. Preparation and execution involves positioning and employing IRC assets in accordance with the IO working group synchronization plan to create desired effects at the right place and time. Assessment involves determining whether planned effects were achieved and recommending adjustments, as necessary.

1-26. The IO officer, IO working group, and the assistant chief of staff, intelligence (G-2/S-2), especially, contribute to the assessment. The IO officer prepares the IO portion of the assessment plan. The IO working group monitors execution of the assessment plan and compares desired results with actual results. The G-2 (S-2), in coordination with the assistant chief of staff, operations (G-3/S-3), contributes by ensuring collection assets are available and tasked to gather information needed to validate measure of effectiveness.

ARMY-JOINT RELATIONSHIPS

1-27. IO, by its nature, is joint. Based on the theater campaign plan, each service component contributes to an integrated whole synchronized by the joint force headquarters. Army IO supports joint force missions two ways. The first is when Army or land component command IRCs are specifically tasked to support a joint force mission. The second is when the Army or land component command, in its support of the joint force, develops its own IO plan, specific to its mission and area of operations. In both instances, IRCs are synchronized across the joint force to create desired effects in and through the information environment, as well as prevent the diminishment or negation of one IRC's effects by another. In multinational operations, the U.S. joint force commander is responsible for coordinating the integration of U.S. IO with multinational information activities.

1-28. The IO officer at joint force headquarters (J-39) synchronizes joint IO efforts. All component commands participate in a synchronization process to maximize effects in the information environment. The process is informed by an IO working group, cell, or virtual center that delivers its recommendations to various decision-making boards. Examples include the Joint Targeting Coordination Board and Joint Intelligence Collection Board. The J-39 provides a staff capability that synchronizes all service-specific IRCs to achieve unity of effort in support of the joint force. Army forces submit requests for IRC or IO unit support and deconfliction measures through multiple channels to higher echelons. For example, requests may go through the J-6 for spectrum management, through liaison at the Air Operations Center for electronic warfare support, through a supporting cyberspace operations center for an effects request, or through the targeting cell for targeting vetting and validation. The J-39 and joint IO cell are kept informed in order to publish plans and orders depicting, maximizing, and assessing mutual support mechanisms for the joint force commander.

INFORMATION OPERATIONS ACROSS THE RANGE OF MILITARY OPERATIONS

1-29. Army forces conduct IO within joint force parameters. From peace to war, and across the range of military operations, commanders integrate and synchronize IO to focus combat power and gain advantage in the information environment. In all situations, Army forces do not act in isolation. Army forces conduct operations in support of a larger joint or multinational plan. Figure 1-1, on page 1-6, depicts the three main categories of military operations within the range of military operations construct:

- Military engagement, security cooperation, and deterrence.
- Crisis response and limited contingency operations.
- Major operations and campaigns.

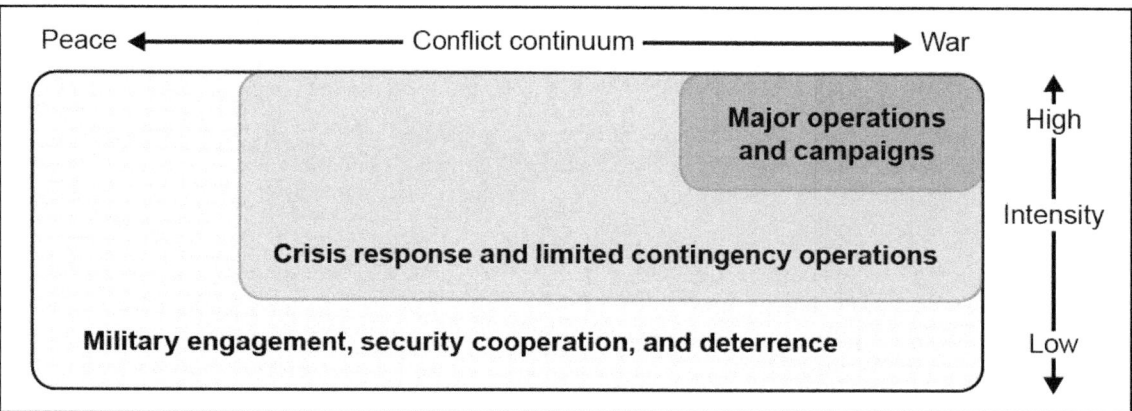

Figure 1-1. The range of military operations across the conflict continuum

MILITARY ENGAGEMENT, SECURITY COOPERATION, AND DETERRENCE

1-30. Military engagement, security cooperation, and deterrence operations are ongoing and recurring military activities that establish, shape, maintain, and refine relations with other nations and domestic civil authorities. The general objective is to protect U.S. interests at home and abroad. IO contributes significantly to military engagement, security cooperation, and deterrence. Military engagement and security cooperation depend heavily on influencing partners and potential partners to align with U.S. interests and, thereby, prevent threats from achieving objectives in or through these same partners and the countries and regions they inhabit. Military engagement and security cooperation are themselves forms of deterrence, but other forms are possible. Deterrence is not only the actual capacity to harm another state or non-state entity who fails to comply with or accommodate U.S. demands, but also the perception of that entity that the U.S. has the ability to do harm, if provoked. IO provides essential support to the shaping and maintaining of this perception through, among other things, the protection of friendly information (OPSEC).

1-31. Complementing IO support to military engagement, security cooperation, and deterrence, as well as crisis response, contingency operations and major operations and campaigns is the Attack the Network framework. This framework consists of activities that employ lethal and nonlethal means to support friendly networks, influence neutral networks, and neutralize threat networks. Since the aim of this framework and the purpose of IO are highly similar, commanders ensure their close coordination. (See ATP 3-90.37 for more information).

CRISIS AND LIMITED CONTINGENCY OPERATIONS

1-32. Contingencies and crisis response operations may be single small-scale, limited-duration operations or a significant part of a major operation of extended duration involving combat. General objectives are to protect U.S. interests and prevent surprise attack or further conflict. These operations typically occur during periods of slightly increased U.S. military readiness, and the use or threat of force may be more probable. Many of these operations involve a combination of military forces in close cooperation with other organizations. Examples include counter-terrorism operations; counter-proliferation; sanctions enforcement; noncombatant evacuation operations; peacekeeping and peace enforcement operations; show of force; strikes and raids; and support to counterinsurgency.

1-33. Army forces conduct IO in accordance with existing contingency or crisis action plans (see JP 5-0). A potential or actual contingency requires commanders at all echelons to gather additional information and refine their contingency plans based on a specific area of operations or target set. Geographic combatant commanders may use the relationships and conditions in the information environment created during peace to influence threat decision makers to act in ways that will resolve the crisis peacefully. Other IO efforts may attempt to influence actors within a target group's political, economic, military, and social structures. Operational and tactical commanders prepare for IO as part of their deployment preparations. They coordinate preparations with the joint force commander to ensure unity of effort and prevent *information fratricide*, **which is defined as adverse effects on the information environment resulting from a failure to effectively synchronize the employment of multiple information-related capabilities which may impede the conduct of friendly operations or adversely affect friendly forces.**

1-34. The objectives during crisis are to halt escalation and move the level of conflict back towards peace. Therefore, commanders conduct IO to develop the situation and refine their situational understanding. Through the deliberate selection and effective synchronization of IRCs, commanders increase the potential that adversaries or other relevant decision makers will choose alternatives other than conflict or war.

MAJOR OPERATIONS AND CAMPAIGNS

1-35. Major operations and campaigns are large-scale, sustained combat operations to achieve national objectives and protect national interests. Such operations may place the United States in a wartime state and are normally conducted against a capable enemy with the will to employ that capability in opposition to or in a manner threatening national security. Major operations may be part of a joint campaign comprised of multiple phases. The goal is to achieve national objectives and conclude hostilities with conditions favorable to the United States and its multinational partners, generally as quickly, with as few casualties as possible, and in a manner that conveys continuing strategic advantage for the United States and its partners.

1-36. During major operations and campaigns, commanders conduct IO to achieve decisive effects in and through the information environment against enemy forces. Well-synchronized IO planning and operational integration supports offense, defense, and stability tasks by weighting IO efforts appropriate to each task. For example, during offense, units conduct IO attack, defend, and stabilize actions, in appropriate combination, to help defeat and destroy enemy forces and capabilities, especially those that are information-related. Units also conduct IO to deny aspects of the information environment (physical, informational, and cognitive) that facilitate threat decision making, while preserving critical information infrastructure, content, and networks essential to friendly decision making.

SECTION III – INFORMATION OPERATIONS AND COMBAT POWER

1-37. The information element of combat power is integral to optimizing combat power, particularly given the increasing relevance of operations in and through the information environment to achieve decisive outcomes. IO and the information element of combat power are related but not the same.

1-38. Information is a resource. As a resource, it must be obtained, developed, refined, distributed, and protected. IO, along with knowledge management and information management, are the ways that units harness this resource and ensure its availability, as well as operationalize and optimize it.

1-39. IO, a component of the mission command warfighting function, supports all other warfighting functions and makes each one more potent. The effects that IO achieves in the information environment amplify the effects of movement and maneuver, intelligence, fires, sustainment and protection, both constructive and destructive.

MISSION COMMAND

1-40. The mission command warfighting function enables commanders to balance the art of command and the science of control in order to integrate the other warfighting functions. It also enables a shared understanding of an operational environment and the commander's intent. IO's focus on protecting information, information systems, and decision making, enhances commanders' ability to integrate the other warfighting functions and create necessary shared understanding. At the same time, it seeks to degrade the enemy's decision-making ability.

1-41. IO supports the accomplishment of several mission command warfighting tasks, including inform and influence audiences inside and outside an organization, conduct knowledge management and information management, synchronize IRCs, and conduct cyberspace electromagnetic activities. Informing and influencing are effects that occur in the cognitive dimension of the information environment. By effectively synchronizing IRCs and, when appropriate, conducting cyberspace electromagnetic activities, commanders tailor their influence and manner of informing to the situation and audience at hand. Information and knowledge management support the commander and staff's ability to access information quickly and completely, as well as segment and protect information, thereby enhancing their decision making and gaining advantage over adversaries and enemies.

MOVEMENT AND MANEUVER

1-42. The movement and maneuver warfighting function moves and employs forces to achieve a position of relative advantage over the enemy through direct fire and close combat. IO seeks to influence or affect enemy decision making so that relative advantage is achieved even before close combat becomes necessary or diminishes the potency of threat actions so that they ultimately fail. Movement and maneuver, along with fires, always produce effects in the information environment, whether intentional or not, and these effects must be considered when planning operations (not just IO). At the same time, movement and maneuver can itself serve as an IRC when its chief objective is to send a message and influence behavior, such as when it is tied to a deception effort.

INTELLIGENCE

1-43. Intelligence facilitates understanding the threat, terrain, and civil considerations. IO enhances and sharpens focus on the aspects of the information environment that influence or are influenced by the threat, such as the threat's IRCs. IO also enhances understanding of the ways that messages are received, transmitted and processed by relevant audiences in the area of operations. In turn, intelligence supports IO by collecting information essential to defining the information environment, understanding the threat's information capabilities, and assessing and adjusting information-related effects.

FIRES

1-44. Fires provides collective and coordinated use of Army indirect fires, air and missile defense, and joint fires through the targeting process. IO effects are typically indirect rather than direct and like indirect fire, greatly benefit from deliberate selection, development and delivery. This fact is why IO targets, like offensive cyberspace operations and space targets, are a part of the targeting process and get nominated to the targeting board for approval.

SUSTAINMENT

1-45. Sustainment provides support and services to ensure freedom of action, extend operational reach, and prolong endurance. IO, through the synchronization of IRCs, seeks to ensure freedom of action in the information environment which, in turn, contributes to enhanced mental and emotional endurance, not just of U.S. forces and their partners, but also of the indigenous populations affected by operations. While morale is a leadership function, it is facilitated through the preservation and sustainment of information, information systems, content, and flow and the ability of leaders to create shared understanding and purpose. Sustainment support and services, such as air dropping supplies to displaced persons or providing health service support, often contribute to effects in the information environment, making coordination between the IO officer and the assistant chief of staff, logistics or G-4 (S-4) essential.

PROTECTION

1-46. The protection warfighting function preserves the force so that commanders can apply maximum combat power to accomplish the mission. IO is focused on the preservation of decision making and ensuring decision-oriented information is available at the right time and place. This means more than simply blunting or preventing the effectiveness of the threat's access to information; it means securing and defending our own.

Chapter 2

Information Operations and Decisive Action

2-1. Unified land operations applies land power as part of unified action to defeat the threat on land and establish conditions that achieve the joint force commander's end state. Combat power is the primary means by which Army forces apply land power. IO synchronization supports combat power by harnessing the information element to optimize the warfighting functions and leadership. In turn, this optimization enables commanders to seize the initiative through decisive action.

2-2. *Decisive action* is the continuous, simultaneous combination of offensive, defensive, and stability or defense support of civil authorities tasks (ADRP 3-0). IO contributes to decisive action through the continuous and simultaneous combination and synchronization of IRCs in support of offense, defense, and stability tasks. IO itself is not offensive, defensive, or stabilizing, but contributes to all of these simultaneously by weighting its efforts in such a way that it achieves requisite effects in and through the information environment in support of the commander's intent.

2-3. To support decisive action effectively, the commander and staff undertake three enabling activities—analyze and depict the information environment, determine IRCs and IO organizations available, and optimize IRC effects. These activities start with understanding and visualizing the information environment in all its complexity. They progress to determining the array of IRCs and IO organizations available to affect the information environment. They culminate with optimizing IRC effects through effective planning, preparation, execution and assessment (see paragraphs 2-12 to 2-22 for a detailed discussion of these enabling activities).

WEIGHTED EFFORTS

2-4. IO weighted efforts are broad orientations used to focus the integration and synchronization of IRCs to create effects that seize, retain, and exploit the initiative in the information environment. Commanders, supported by their staffs, visualize and describe how IO will support the concept of operations by aligning and balancing the efforts of defend, attack, and stabilize with corresponding decisive action tasks as shown in figure 2-1 on page 2-2.

IO WEIGHTED EFFORT: DEFEND

2-5. When the IO effort necessitates a defend orientation, it seeks to create effects in the information environment that accomplish any one or combination of the following (not all inclusive):
- Physical dimension.
  - Locking or otherwise physically securing documents, equipment and infrastructure that facilitate decision making.
  - Protecting documents, equipment, and structures from destruction or degradation.
  - Protecting key personnel from attack or exploitation.
  - Using obscurants to mask movements.
- Informational dimension.
  - Encrypting communications.
  - Preserving the free-flow of information and access to data and information sources.
  - Employing knowledge management principles.
  - Proactively identifying instances of social engineering or malware and keeping virus and other protections current.
  - Using forensics to determine sources of attack.

- ▪ Countering enemy or adversary information efforts.
- ● Cognitive dimension.
  - ▪ Making decentralized decisions.
  - ▪ Checking facts and assumptions.
  - ▪ Using precedents or best practices.
  - ▪ Using red teaming.

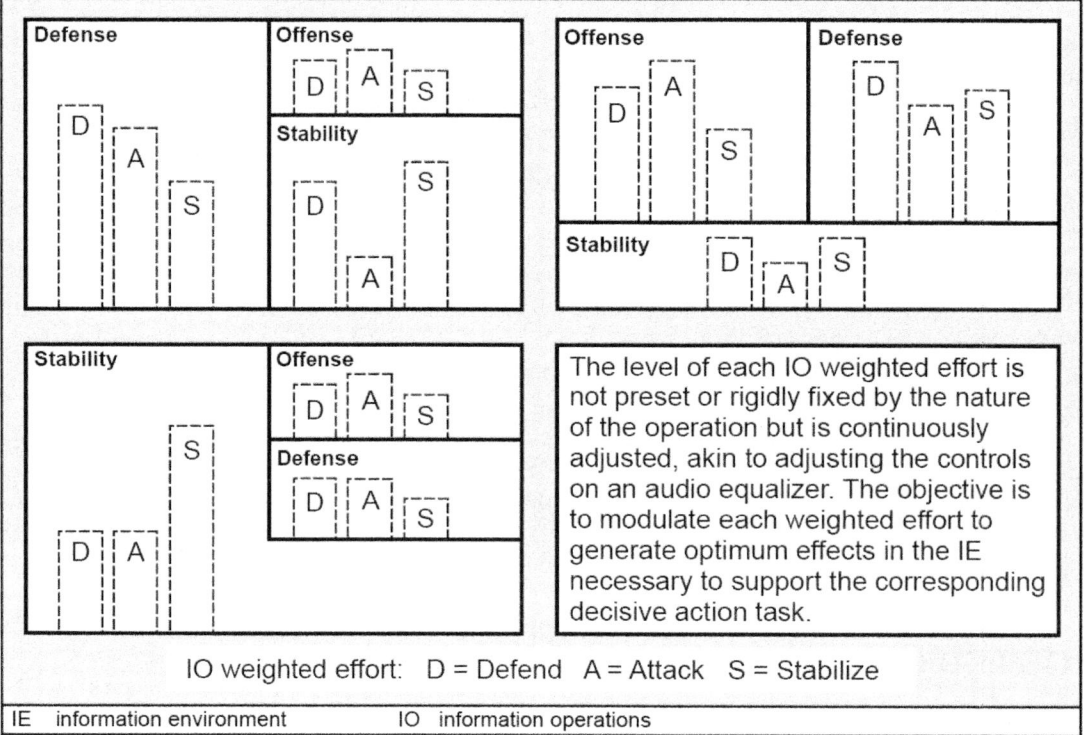

Figure 2-1. IO weighted efforts

2-6. IRCs that are most often synchronized to achieve a defend orientation in the information environment include, but are not limited to:

- ● Cyberspace operations.
- ● Electronic warfare.
- ● Military deception.
- ● MISO.
- ● Operations security (OPSEC).
- ● Physical security.
- ● Destruction and lethal actions.
- ● Special technical operations.

IO WEIGHTED EFFORT: ATTACK

2-7. When the IO effort necessitates an attack orientation, it seeks to create effects in the information environment that accomplish any one or combination of the following (not all inclusive):

- ● Physical dimension.
  - ▪ Destroying or degrading threat command and control (C2) systems.
  - ▪ Degrading or destroying threat leadership.
  - ▪ Destroying or impairing threat networks and critical nodes (human or infrastructure).

- Using feints, ruses, demonstrations, and displays.
- Informational dimension.
  - Jamming communication and signals.
  - Corrupting data and information.
  - Employing denial of service attacks.
  - Intercepting or misdirecting data or content.
  - Manipulating information provided to adversary leaders.
  - Attacking the enemy's or adversary's narrative(s).
  - Using social engineering or spoofing.
- Cognitive dimension.
  - Creating ambiguity or confusion.
  - Causing an incorrect understanding of friendly intent.
  - Creating hesitancy or procrastination.
  - Enabling overconfidence in false signals and signs; under confidence or uncertainty in the true ones.
  - Degrading support for the threat.
  - Degrading legitimacy of threat narrative(s).

2-8. IRCs that are most often synchronized to achieve an attack orientation in the information environment include, but are not limited to:

- Cyberspace operations.
- Electronic warfare.
- Military deception.
- MISO.
- Destruction and lethal actions.
- Special technical operations.
- Space operations.
- Soldier and leader engagement (SLE).

IO WEIGHTED EFFORT: STABILIZE

2-9. When the IO effort necessitates a stabilize orientation, it seeks to create effects in the information environment that accomplish any one or combination of the following (not all inclusive):

- Physical dimension.
  - Meeting with key leaders, decision makers, or people who can influence the behaviors of others.
  - Visibly demonstrating mutual commitment or support.
  - Establishing, supporting and utilizing new infrastructure or media that increases or enhances quantity and quality of communication between U.S.-led forces and relevant audiences.
  - Identifying and cultivating traditional or indigenous communicators.
  - Aligning Soldier and unit actions with their words and images.
- Informational dimension.
  - Employing audience- and culturally-attuned messages.
  - Countering threat or adversary information efforts and narratives through coordinated actions.
  - Aligning images and words with unit and individual Soldier actions.
  - Using messages crafted by native speakers and communicators.
  - Nesting messages with higher headquarters themes and messages and strategic communication guidance.
- Cognitive dimension.
  - Creating support for rule of law, local security forces, and legitimate authority.

- Enhancing understanding of U.S. operations and desired outcomes.
- Changing perceptions, attitudes, and, ultimately, behaviors.

2-10. The IRCs that are most often synchronized to achieve a stabilize orientation in the information environment include, but are not limited to:

- Combat camera.
- MISO.
- Presence, posture and profile.
- Public affairs.
- Civil affairs operations and civil military operations.
- SLE, including police engagement.
- OPSEC.
- Foreign disclosure.

IO AND DEFENSE SUPPORT OF CIVIL AUTHORITIES

2-11. IO does not participate in defense support of civil authorities. However, if requested by civil authorities and approved by the Secretary of Defense, select IRCs may support civil authorities in the conduct of their operations.

IO ENABLING ACTIVITIES

2-12. To support decisive action, as well as accomplish IO's purpose, commanders, staffs, and in particular, the IO officer or representative, undertake and accomplish three enabling activities:

- Analyze and depict the information environment in all its complexity.
- Determine the array of IRCs and IO organizations (such as Theater IO Groups) available to affect the information environment and the advantages each offers.
- Optimize the effects of IRCs through effective planning, preparation, execution, and assessment.

ANALYZE AND DEPICT THE INFORMATION ENVIRONMENT

2-13. To achieve advantage in the information environment, commanders, with specialized advice and support from the IO officer, ensure that IO planning is fully integrated into the operations process. This begins with analysis to understand, visualize, and describe the information environment.

2-14. A significant part of what makes the operational environment complex is the information environment because it includes such components as cyberspace, the electromagnetic spectrum, data flow, encryption and decryption, the media, biases, perceptions, decisions, key leaders and decision makers, among many others. What occurs in the physical dimension of the information environment and, more broadly, the operational environment, always has second- and third-order effects in the informational and cognitive dimensions of the information environment. Thus, there must be holistic and nuanced understanding of how these various components and dimensions interrelate and the whole operates.

2-15. This understanding is depicted through a series of information overlays and comprehensive combined information overlays, which vary depending on commanders' priorities, the nature of the operation, and the type of analysis being conducted. Modeling or mapping social or human networks also enhances this understanding. While complex, the information environment still needs to be captured in a way that the commander can visualize and understand it, draw necessary insights and conclusions, and make informed decisions. The IO officer should not be locked into any specific method for analyzing and depicting the information environment but develop a process and overlays that best serve the commander and, as appropriate, follow unit standard operating procedures. As new technologies and interactive capabilities emerge, they should be incorporated as tools to facilitate the visualization and understanding processes.

DETERMINE IRCs AND IO ORGANIZATIONS AVAILABLE

2-16. The IO officer is the staff focal point for information environment analysis and expertise, as well as IRC synchronization. The two are inextricably linked: effective IRC synchronization can only occur when the information environment is understood fully. Additionally, effective IRC synchronization can also only occur when a single entity can look across all IRCs and articulate their contribution to the fight and how they can mutually support each other. The IO officer, located in the assistant chief of staff, operations (G-3/S-3) staff section, in concert with the IO working group, is this synchronization entity. Three key responsibilities of the IO officer, therefore, are to build rapport with IRC units, determine ways to optimize each IRC's contribution through synchronization, and facilitate IRC operations and activities by coordinating support for them, while minimizing impediments.

2-17. In addition to building rapport with IRC units, the IO officer must build similar rapport with and knowledge of IO organizations available and the ways they augment and enhance the function's effectiveness. These units include the 1st IO Command (Land) and the reserve component regionally-aligned Theater IO Groups.

2-18. The IO officer also continually assesses whether the necessary assets and capabilities are available to achieve the commander's intent and concept of operations. If it is determined that augmentation—by specific IRCs or by IO units—is necessary, the IO officer or appropriate IRC representative requests augmentation or determines alternative courses of action to fulfill its scheme of IO and meet mission objectives.

2-19. Information-related organizations and entities also exist within the interagency and among Unified Action partners. IO officers not only must know these organizations and entities, they must invite their participation whenever feasible, particularly through their ad hoc or habitual membership in the IO working group, which coordinates, synchronizes, and deconflicts the information-related efforts of these partner organizations with its own efforts.

OPTIMIZE IRC EFFECTS

2-20. Optimizing IRC effects begins in earnest with receipt of mission and continues throughout the operations process. With information environment analysis and understanding already accounted for, other IO officer tasks necessary to ensure effective IRC synchronization and the optimization of their effects are:

- Participate in the military decisionmaking process (MDMP) and develop the scheme of IO.
- Convene and chair the IO working group.
- Work closely with IRC units and IO units to ensure capabilities are positioned, employed, and supported to fulfill the synchronization plan.
- Integrate targets within the information environment into the targeting process and develop, maintain and update IRC synchronization matrix.
- Coordinate and deconflict IRC synchronization with public affairs efforts to ensure unity of effort and compliance with legal and policy limitations and exclusions.
- Assess IO and IRC effectiveness in achieving planned effects and adjust as necessary.

Other books we publish on Amazon.com

DDI-1120-129-76

DEFENSE INTELLIGENCE AGENCY

DIR
Defense
Intelligence
Report

SOVIET TANK
COMPANY TACTICS

MAY 1976

Chapter 3

Roles, Responsibilities, Relationships, and Organizations

3-1. Every member of a unit—from the commander, to the staff, to the IO officer or representative, to individual Soldiers and Army civilians—contributes to IO. Also essential to mission success are the IRCs supporting the unit's IO efforts, as well as any augmenting IO units. Each has a specific role and important responsibilities to fulfill or undertake, as well as vital relationships to forge and sustain, in order to achieve advantage in and through the information environment.

THE COMMANDER

3-2. Commanders, at all levels, are responsible for knowing what threats their units face and how to exploit or defeat them. They are their unit's chief influencers and engage relevant audiences and actors, as necessary, to shape the information environment to their advantage. Commanders rely on their staff and IO officer, in particular, to assist in planning, preparing, executing, and assessing IO. They also personally direct and review analysis of the information environment, issue guidance on the employment and synchronization of IRCs, and direct adjustments based on assessment results.

3-3. Cognizant of the pervasive impact of the information environment on operations and the need to affect this environment to their advantage, commanders are mindful of the following:

- Every operation has, to some degree, an effect on the information environment.
- IO planning is integral to operations from the start.
- Effects in and through the information environment, if essential to success, are part of the commander's intent.
- Combat power cannot be optimized without IO.
- The warfighting functions (particularly movement and maneuver and fires) produce effects in the information environment, whether intentional or not.
- IO is essential to operational success at all levels, whether or not the unit has an assigned IO officer.
- All communication can quickly become global and have strategic consequences.
- IRCs can have lengthy lead times to coordinate and employ, as well as lengthy lag times before their effects are realized.
- The alignment of words, deeds, and images is essential to building trust and confidence with relevant audiences in the area of operations.
- IO requires prioritized intelligence support.
- Effects in the information environment are not always caused as expected; assessment is difficult and benefits from commanders' interest, prioritization and support.
- U.S. IO can be constrained by policy and law, while the threat is often unconstrained in its use of information.

THE STAFF

3-4. Each staff section collaborates routinely, but to varying degrees, with the IO officer to plan, synchronize, support, and assess IO. Representatives from the G-2 (S-2), G-3 (S-3), assistant chief of staff, plans G-5 (S-5), assistant chief of staff, signal G-6 (S-6) and assistant chief of staff, civil affairs operations (G-9/S-9), in particular, serve as core members of the IO working group.

ASSISTANT CHIEF OF STAFF, G-1 (S-1), PERSONNEL

3-5. The G-1 (S-1) is the principal staff officer for personnel functions. The G-1 (S-1) processes requirements for individual, team and unit augmentation or attachment. It coordinates reception of these individuals, teams, or units and validates their requirements. It also builds manning documents, as required. Additional IO-related responsibilities include, but are not limited to:

- Designating a representative to the IO working group.
- Providing IO-focused instructions in the personnel appendix of the sustainment annex.
- Reviewing the IO mission and mission, enemy, terrain and weather, troops and support available, time available, and civil considerations from a personnel support perspective.

ASSISTANT CHIEF OF STAFF, G-2 (S-2), INTELLIGENCE

3-6. The G-2 (S-2) is the principal staff officer for all matters concerning military intelligence, security operations, and military intelligence training. The G-2 (S-2) produces the intelligence used by the IO officer, element, working group and IRCs. IO-related responsibilities of the G-2 (S-2) include, but are not limited to:

- Participating as a core member of the IO working group and providing intelligence briefings or updates.
- Providing IO-focused instructions in the intelligence annex.
- Including requests for information from the IO officer in intelligence reach.
- Answering information requirements (IRs) submitted by the IO officer.
- Coordinating with counterintelligence; law enforcement; and information system developers, providers, administrators, and users to ensure timely sharing of relevant information.
- Preparing a threat assessment of enemy command and control systems, including:
  - Political, economic, social, and cultural influences.
  - Targets and methods for offensive operations.
  - Enemy decision-making processes.
  - Biographical backgrounds of key threat leaders, decision makers, and communicators, and their advisors. Including motivating factors and leadership styles.
  - A comprehensive comparison of enemy offensive information capabilities against friendly IO vulnerabilities.
- Collecting data to establish an electronic warfare database and command and control target list.
- Providing intelligence support to military deception operations; specifically:
  - Helping the G-6 (S-6) plan use of friendly information systems as deception means.
  - Establishing counterintelligence measures to protect the military deception operation from detection.

ASSISTANT CHIEF OF STAFF, G-3 (S-3), OPERATIONS

3-7. The G-3 (S-3) is the principal staff officer for all matters concerning training and leader development, operations and plans, and force development modernization. IO-related responsibilities include, but are not limited to:

- Exercising primary responsibility for IO staff functions and overseeing the IO officer, who is part of the movement and maneuver cell.
- With assistance from the IO officer, integrating IO planning into the military decisionmaking process.
- Validating or approving, as necessary, IO officer inputs, actions and outputs. Among the inputs and outputs, the mission statement, scheme of IO, and IO objectives require G-3 (S-3) review, refinement, and emphasis.
- If additional IRCs or IO units are required, prioritizing and facilitating the augmentation request or request for forces.
- Tasking units and assets necessary to achieve IO objectives.

- Providing plans and current operations briefings to IO working group meetings.
- Integrating information collection into operations, supported by the G-2 (S-2).
- Ensuring effective coordination and synchronization among the IO officer and IRC staff representatives and other members of the IO working group.

ASSISTANT CHIEF OF STAFF, G-4 (S-4), LOGISTICS

3-8. The G-4 (S-4) is the principal staff officer for all matters concerning sustainment operations. IO-related responsibilities of the G-4 (S-4) include, but are not limited to:

- Ensuring required resources are included on the baseline resources item list and the commander's track item list.
- Coordinating sustainment per priorities and requirements.
- Tracking the operational readiness of IO units and equipment.
- Providing sustainment capability or vulnerability input to the IO estimate and course of action analyses.
- Advising the deception and IO working groups on how military operations will affect logistics personnel and equipment.
- Designating a representative to the IO working group.
- Providing IO-focused instruction in the sustainment annex.

ASSISTANT CHIEF OF STAFF, G-5 (S-5), PLANS

3-9. The G-5 (S-5) is responsible for incorporating future plans into ongoing operations. The IO officer works closely with the G-5 (S-5) to ensure its efforts to affect the information environment support future plans and provide the commander necessary freedom of action to sustain the initiative and achieve decisive results. When required, the G-5 (S-5) and IO officer work closely to plan and implement deception efforts and ensure objectives are incorporated effectively into plans and operations orders.

ASSISTANT CHIEF OF STAFF, G-6 (S-6), SIGNAL

3-10. The G-6 (S-6) is the principal staff officer for all matters concerning Department of Defense information network operations (also called DODIN operations), applicable portions of defensive cyberspace operations, network transport, information services, and spectrum management operations within the unit's area of operations. IO-related responsibilities of the G-6 (S-6) include but are not limited to:

- Coordinating information management with and providing information management data to the G-3 (S-3).
- Providing a representative to the IO working group.
- Providing IO-related instructions in relevant annexes and appendices.
- Directing the actions of subordinate DODIN operations and information management staff elements.
- Coordinating DODIN operations and information management support of information collection with the G-2 (S-2).
- Coordinating with the Army Cyber Operations and Integration Center for antivirus software and threat analysis and advisories, after receiving notification of its support from the G-3 (S-3).
- Coordinating with the regional cyber center for network intrusion devices, information, approved systems, and software, after receiving notification of its support from the G-3 (S-3).

ASSISTANT CHIEF OF STAFF, G-9 (S-9), CIVIL AFFAIRS OPERATIONS

3-11. The G-9 (S-9) is the principal staff officer for all matters concerning civil affairs and civil military operations. The G-9 (S-9) evaluates civil considerations within missions and identifies centers of gravity that are civil in nature. IO-related responsibilities of the G-9 (S-9) include, but are not limited to:

- Providing a G-9 (S-9) representative to the IO working group.
- Providing IO-focused instructions in the civil affairs operations annex.

- Interfacing with IO officer on the use of civil military operations in support of the scheme of IO.
- Identifying and procuring civilian resources to support the scheme of IO.
- Advising the military deception officer of implications of military deception operations on civil affairs operations.
- Coordinating with the IO and psychological operations officers on trends in public sentiments.
- Coordinating with the IO officer, public affairs officer, and psychological operations officer to ensure messages are not contradictory.

THE IO OFFICER

3-12. The IO officer (who heads the IO element at division and higher) or representative (at brigade and below) is the staff focal point for IO. The IO officer is responsible for the following specific tasks, among others:

- Analyzing the information environment to discern impacts it will have on unit operations and to exploit opportunities to gain an advantage over threat forces.
- Identifying the most effective IRCs to achieve objectives.
- Synchronizing IRCs to achieve objectives in the information environment.
- Assessing the risk, typically described as risk to mission and risk to force, associated with the employment of any capability, product, program or message.
- Providing input to the synchronization matrix for the use of available IRCs in support of unit operations.
- Identifying IRC gaps not resolvable at the unit level.
- Coordinating with other Army, Service, or joint forces to use IRCs to augment existing unit capability shortfalls.
- Providing information as required in support of operations security (OPSEC) at the unit level.
- Providing information as required in support of military deception at the unit level.
- Leading the IO working group.
- Assessing the effectiveness of employed IRCs.

3-13. The IO officer contributes to the overall intelligence preparation of the battlefield (IPB) by assisting the G-2 (S-2) in identifying and evaluating threat information capabilities, as well as the means to influence the population. Additionally, the IO officer submits to the G-2 (S-2) any IRs regarding intelligence shortfalls about the information environment and coordinates with the G-2 (S-2) in developing templates, databases, and other relevant products, including but not limited to:

- Religion, language, and culture of key groups and decision makers.
- Agendas of nongovernmental organizations.
- Size and location of threat IO or information warfare forces and assets.
- Military and civilian communication infrastructures and connectivity.
- Population demographics, linkages, and related information.
- Audio, video, and print media outlets and centers and the populations they service.
- Location and types of electromagnetic systems and emitters.
- Network vulnerabilities of friendly, neutral, and threat forces.

3-14. Additional tasks for which the IO officer is responsible include, but are not limited to:

- Participating in the military decisionmaking process.
- Developing IRs.
- Producing information and combined information overlays.
- Developing the scheme of IO.
- Through commander's communication synchronization, contribute to development of the commander's narrative.
- Integrating IO into the unit's targeting process.
- Deconflicting the employment of IRCs.

- Ensuring IO-related information is updated in the common operational picture.
- Integrating external augmentation.

3-15. Not all units are authorized an IO officer or element. Commanders may, therefore, adapt their staff structure to ensure IO objectives and IRC tasks are accomplished and appoint an officer or non-commissioned officer to perform the duties of the IO officer, outlined in this manual. Task organizing for IO is situation-, mission- and commander-dependent.

3-16. A key responsibility of the IO officer is to understand the command relationship with IRC units and build rapport accordingly. Building rapport typically begins with a visit to the IRC site location, an orientation on the IRC's potential contributions and limitations, and a collaborative determination of ways to optimize the IRC's effects with other IRCs through synchronization. This rapport-building is ongoing and primarily channeled through the IO working group, although one-on-one conversations will also occur.

3-17. When necessary, the IO officer must be ready to lead the planning and employment of select IRCs not clearly managed by a capability owner or proponent. Examples include, but are not limited to: military deception; OPSEC; and Presence, Posture, and Profile. The IO officer is also ready to coordinate for and integrate IRCs that are only found at higher echelons, such as cyberspace operations.

INFORMATION-RELATED CAPABILITIES

3-18. IO seeks to optimize the combined effects of selected IRCs through effective planning, synchronization, and assessment. While a single IRC can affect the information environment to friendly advantage, synchronized IRC activities and operations can amplify and unify each other's effects and produce more efficacious and durable results. For example, variation and repetition of actions and messages tends to increase their overall effect, if not their acceptance. Using different IRCs, in combination, to execute actions and deliver messages, provides this requisite variation.

3-19. IRCs are diverse. In some cases, they are part of the force structure, such as military information support operations (MISO) units, civil affairs units, or combat camera units. Coordination of these IRCs will be with the IRC unit commander, G-3 (S-3), or designed representative. In other cases, IRCs are tasks or activities managed by a staff section, such as military deception, OPSEC, or special technical operations. Coordination of these IRCs will occur with the staff element's director or a specified action officer.

3-20. All IRCs units work collaboratively with the IO officer, as well as with other IRCs, to facilitate their synchronization into the IO portion of the concept of operations, also called the scheme of IO. They do this primarily through the IO working group but utilize any venue or engagement to advance their capability's contribution to the total effort. Most importantly, they articulate their capability's strengths, limitations, and risks to the commander and staff to facilitate decision making about their employment and synchronization.

INFORMATION OPERATIONS SUPPORT UNITS

3-21. The G-3 (S-3), with the assistance of the IO officer, and in concert with organic IRCs, serves as the entry point for external IRCs (excluding public affairs) and IO support units, assets and resources and ensures their integration into overall planning, preparation, execution, and assessment. Among the support organizations that the IO officer helps the G-3 (S-3) to integrate are the 1st Information Operations Command (Land) (1st IO Command) and the reserve component theater information operations groups, which provide a range of IO subject-matter expertise, skills augmentation, and reachback.

1ST INFORMATION OPERATIONS COMMAND (LAND)

3-22. The 1st IO Command, a major subordinate command of the U.S. Army Intelligence and Security Command, is a brigade-sized, multi-compo unit. Under the operational control and tasking authority of the U.S. Army Cyber Command, it provides uniquely tailored IO and cyberspace operations (CO) planning, synchronization, assessment, and reachback support to the Army and other military forces. Consisting of a Headquarters and Headquarters Detachment and two battalions, it augments military forces with tailored IO and cyberspace operations support provided through deployable teams, opposing forces support, reachback planning and analysis, and specialized training to assist units in garrison, during exercises, and during contingency operations.

3-23. 1st IO Command also supports the Army by working to optimize IO interoperability with joint forces, other military forces, inter-agencies, and allies. It provides expeditionary cyberspace operations support to help units identify network vulnerabilities and enable IO.

Deployable Modular IO Teams

3-24. Deploys a variety of mission-tailored IO and cyberspace operations teams. The configuration of each deploying team varies to meet operational requirements.

Field Support Team

3-25. Provides IO subject-matter expertise to supported commands to assist with the planning, execution and assessment of IO during crisis, contingency, and exercise operations. Field support team members are trained in the operational integration of military deception, electronic warfare, MISO, OPSEC, cyberspace operations, and other activities impacting the information environment.

Vulnerability Assessment Team

3-26. Assists supported commands in identifying and resolving IO and cyberspace vulnerabilities in order to improve the command's defensive posture. The vulnerability assessment teams deploy to provide either: Train and Assist (Blue Team) or Emulation of an Adversarial Attack (Red Team) support. Both are capable of assessing the supported command's OPSEC, physical security, and electronic security training and policies to identify vulnerabilities. Both vulnerability assessment teams also assist the supported command in identifying IO and cyberspace vulnerabilities tied to issues associated with unit procedures, equipment, and other resources, and in finding means to resolve or mitigate identified issues. In addition, the vulnerability assessment teams augment the U.S. Army Forces Command mission command assessment teams in conducting pre-deployment home station cybersecurity training, as well as execute the Command Cyber Readiness Inspections for Army Cyber Command in coordination with the Defense Information Systems Agency.

OPSEC Support Team

3-27. The OPSEC support team is part of the 1st IO Command organizational structure, and augments vulnerability assessment teams and executes independent OPSEC support team missions. OPSEC support teams provide supported commands with OPSEC training, assist with developing OPSEC programs, and assess unit OPSEC programs.

World Class Cyber Opposing Force

3-28. Provides cyber and information warfare opposing force support to designated commands during operational training events, such as major exercises and combat training center rotations. This force serves as a non-cooperative, multiple tier (criminal, hybrid, nation state) cyberspace threat opponent that challenges, trains, and develops leaders to successfully operate within a hostile information environment. The World Class Cyber Opposing Force executes its opposing force mission as the exercise dictates, and will operate either as an independent force or as a member of a larger opposing force.

Reachback and Training Support

3-29. Provides IO planning support, intelligence analysis, and technical assistance to deployed 1st IO Command support teams, and to other commands requesting reachback support. Reachback tailors its analytical and intelligence efforts and products to support the current and future operations of the supported commands. Lastly, the reachback provides technical support for the execution of vulnerability assessments and World Class Cyber Opposing Force missions.

3-30. The 1st IO Command conducts training instruction throughout the year on the planning, integration and execution of IRCs in both a resident (at Fort Belvoir) and mobile training team format. The 1st IO

Command deploys mobile training teams to requesting commands and installations to provide IO and cyberspace training. Deployed mobile training teams have the ability to tailor instruction to meet the specific requirements of the requesting command. A list of the 1st IO Command training courses can be found in the Army Training Requirements and Resources System.

THEATER INFORMATION OPERATIONS GROUPS

3-31. The Army relies upon Theater Information Operations Groups to provide enhanced information operations planning, synchronization, and assessment support to Army echelons at theater and army service component command down to brigade level. There are two Theater IO Groups, the 56th and 71st Theater IO Groups, in the U.S. Army National Guard and two Theater IO Groups in the U.S. Army Reserve, the 151st and 152nd Theater IO Groups. Each Theater IO Group consists of a group headquarters, a headquarters and headquarters company, and two IO battalions which mirror each other in their capabilities.

3-32. The mission of the Theater IO Groups is to provide IO subject-matter expertise to a supported command in the form of deployable modular IO teams and a reach back, as well as home station support capability. The Theater IO Groups and its battalion elements do not usually deploy as commands but instead form and deploy purpose-built IO teams designed to provide the necessary IO support required by the requesting command. To enhance the capabilities of the IO teams and reduce preparation time, the Theater IO Groups maintain regional focuses. This focus helps provide the supported command additional regional expertise and capability to plan, synchronize, and assess IRC activities in the conduct of IO within the area of operations. Having a regional focus, however, does not preclude a Theater IO Groups from deploying IO teams and providing IO support to organizations and commands outside of its regional focus area.

Deployable Modular IO Teams

3-33. The Theater IO Groups task organize and deploy mission-focused, modular IO teams created from the various capabilities resident within the Theater IO Groups. In the field, the modular IO teams provide the supported command with IO planning, synchronization, assessment, and analysis of the information environment. These teams have the capability to plan, synchronize, and assess OPSEC and military deception in the supported command. When dictated by mission requirements, the Theater IO Groups S-2 can attach intelligence specialists to a deployed modular IO team. If a modular IO team is not required, Theater IO Groups can deploy individual elements to meet requested mission support focused on planning, synchronization, and assessment of IRCs. In the creation of the modular IO teams, the Theater IO Groups draw upon the expertise resident in the following Theater IO Groups elements.

Army Service Component Command Support Detachment

3-34. Provides the regionally-aligned Army Service Component Command with a culturally-aware, regionally-focused IO planning, synchronization, and assessment capability that can synchronize and assess IO. This detachment provides the supported Army Service Component Command with the expertise to integrate IRCs in concert with other activities into theater security cooperation plans, war plans, and contingency planning. The detachment augments the supported unit's organic IO element or acts as the supported command's IO element. It also serves as the base Theater IO Group element for task organization with other Theater IO Groups capabilities to create a theater, Army Service Component Command-level modular team.

Field Support Detachment

3-35. Provides a culturally-aware, regionally-focused IO planning, synchronization, and assessment capability that can synchronize and assess IO. This detachment provides the supported command with the expertise to integrate IRCs in concert with other activities into operations plans, operations orders, and contingency planning. It can either augment the supported command's G-3 (S-3) IO element or serve as that element. It also serves as the base Theater IO Group element for task organization with other Theater IO Groups capabilities to create a Corps and below modular IO team.

Military Deception Support Detachment

3-36. Equips the supported command with a regionally-aligned military deception-focused planning, coordination, implementation, and assessment capability. Military deception support detachments are trained to identify deception opportunities, deception conduits and means, and develop plans focused on exploiting those opportunities and means. As part of its support functions, the military deception support detachment develops and maintains social-cultural threat databases to include methods and means of communication (conduits) for input to the targeting process. It can either augment or act as the supported command's deception cell.

Assessment Detachments

3-37. Provide multi-disciplined IO effects assessments. They assess the information environment and integrate IO-related collection and assessment into initial planning. They develop criteria in the form of measures of effectiveness and measures of performance and establish indicators for evaluation. Each indicator represents an IR that should identify a set of sources and staff members who collect the information in the assessment plan. Measures of performance and effectiveness are simply criteria—they require relevant information in the form of indicators for evaluation.

OPSEC Support Detachments

3-38. OPSEC support detachments provide planning, synchronization, implementation, and assessment of OPSEC programs to identify friendly critical capabilities, critical vulnerabilities, and critical information in military plans, operations, and supporting activities and prevent exposure to enemy intelligence systems. They determine and advise supported commanders on indicators that threat intelligence systems might obtain that could be interpreted or pieced together to derive critical information in time to be useful to enemies. In concert with other IRCs, they nominate and employ OPSEC measures that eliminate or reduce to an acceptable level, the vulnerabilities of friendly actions to enemy exploitation.

Web OPSEC Support Detachment

3-39. Administers planning, synchronization, implementation and assessment of web-based OPSEC programs to identify friendly critical capabilities, critical vulnerabilities and critical information in military plans, operations, and supporting activities and prevent exposure to enemy intelligence systems. Recommends and advises on OPSEC implications to cyberspace operations.

Reachback and Home Station Support

3-40. The Theater IO Groups maintain an intelligence support capability designed to produce detailed IO-centric analysis of the operational environment and potential threats (infrastructure; key leaders; information systems; IRCs; composition; vulnerabilities; and friendly, neutral, and threat indigenous networks and their relation to each other) in support of deployed teams. The Theater IO Groups also maintain a habitual relationship with intelligence organizations to provide IO-centric support and products. Deployed teams coordinate with the Theater IO Group's S-2 and Intelligence Integration Element for information which is used in the development of courses of action, target analysis, and creation of a combined information overlay.

The Intelligence Integration Element and Other Support

3-41. Contains intelligence specialists who provide multidiscipline intelligence analysis in support of individual Theater IO Groups elements and deployable modular IO teams. Trained on IO in order to provide tailored intelligence support, these specialists can support from home station, deploy to augment command's resident IO element, or as members of an IO team. When deployed, these specialists can serve as the focal point for coordination with other intelligence elements.

3-42. In addition to intelligence reachback support, the Theater IO Groups can also provide technical support from home station through the Army Service Component Command support detachments and the web OPSEC support detachment. The Army Service Component Command support detachments are capable of providing theater support planning from either home station or on site at the supported theater Army Service Component Command headquarters. The web OPSEC support detachment is capable of deploying as part of a modular IO team but more often it provides support from home station where it has assured access to the internet and web based mission command systems.

Note: Commanders can request Theater IO Group's IO team augmentation, reach back support, and home station support by submitting a Request for Forces through their chain of command to their respective Army Service Component Command, where the request for forces will be forwarded to U.S. Army Forces Command for approval. After approval by Forces Command, the request for forces is passed to the National Guard Bureau or the United States Army Reserve for servicing. The employment will consist of mission-tailored and scaled IO teams provided, as needed, to either a single or multiple commands and echelons, or the dedication of the entire IO group to support an Army Service Component Command. In the latter case, the IO group will provide IO support to the Army Service Component Command and its subordinate command structures down to brigade.

56th Theater IO Group: Assigned to the Washington Army National Guard with one battalion located in the Maryland Army National Guard. Regional focus areas are U.S. Pacific Command, U.S. Central Command, and U. S. Northern Command.

71st Theater IO Group: Assigned to the Texas Army National Guard. Regional focus areas are U.S. Southern Command, U.S. Northern Command and U.S. Africa Command.

151st Theater IO Group: Assigned to the U.S. Army Reserve. Regional focus areas are U.S. Africa Command, U.S. European Command, and U.S. Central Command.

152nd Theater IO Group: Assigned to the U.S. Army Reserve. Regional focus areas are U.S. Central Command, U.S. Pacific Command, and U.S. European Command. (To be inactivated FY 2017)

INDIVIDUAL SOLDIERS AND ARMY CIVILIANS

3-43. IO seeks to influence adversaries or enemies, as well as foreign audiences to acquiesce to or support our demands or align their actions in concert with the friendly commander's intent and objectives. One of the most potent and readily-available IRCs to influence these audiences is Soldier and leader engagement. *Soldier and leader engagements* **are interpersonal Service-member interactions with audiences in an area of operations**. When Soldiers and leaders, inclusive of Army civilians and contractors, align their words, images, and actions in support of the commander's communications strategy, they contribute to mission accomplishment in a forceful and enduring way. Additional actions necessary to conduct Soldier and leader engagements include, but are not limited to:

- Knowing and understanding the commander's intent.
- Studying local culture, habits, and ways of communicating.
- Memorizing approved talking points.
- Being alert to non-verbal cues or signals on both sides of any conversation or engagement.
- Following through on commitments.

Other books we publish on Amazon.com

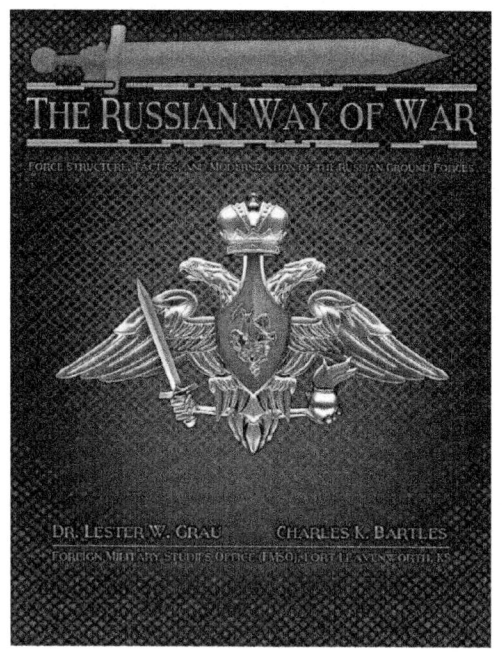

Chapter 4

Planning

4-1. *Planning* is the art and science of understanding a situation, envisioning a desired future, and laying out effective ways of bringing that future about (ADP 5-0). Planning helps commanders create and communicate a common vision between commanders, their staffs, subordinate commanders, and unified action partners. Planning results in a plan and orders that synchronize the action of forces in time, space, and purpose to achieve objectives and accomplish missions.

4-2. Commanders, supported by their staffs, ensure IO is fully integrated into the plan, starting with Army design methodology (ADM) and progressing through the military decisionmaking process (MDMP). The focal point for IO planning is the IO officer (or designated representative for IO). However, the entire staff contributes to planning products that describe and depict how IO supports the commander's intent and concept of operations. The staff also contributes to IO planning during IO working group meetings to include assessing the effectiveness of IO and refining the plan.

PLANNING OVERVIEW

4-3. Planning activities occupy a continuum ranging from conceptual to detailed. Conceptual planning involves understanding operational environments and problems, determining the operation's end state, and visualizing an operational approach to attain that end state. Detailed planning translates the commander's operational approach into a complete and practical plan. Generally, detailed planning is associated with the science of control including synchronizing forces in time, space, and purpose to accomplish missions.

4-4. ADM helps commanders and staffs with the conceptual aspects of planning. These aspects include understanding, visualizing, and describing operations to include framing the problem and identifying an operational approach to solve the problem. The MDMP helps commanders and staffs translate the commander's vision into an operations plan or operations order that synchronizes the actions of the force in time, space, and purpose to accomplish missions. Both the problem the commander needs to solve and the specific operation to advance towards its solution have significant information-related aspects.

IO and Army Design Methodology

4-5. ADM is a methodology for applying critical and creative thinking to understand, visualize, and describe unfamiliar problems and approaches to solving them (ADP 5-0). By first framing an operational environment and associated problems, ADM enables commanders and staffs to think about the situation in depth. From this understanding, commanders and staffs develop a more informed approach to solve or manage identified problems. During operations, ADM supports organizational learning through reframing— a maturing of understanding that leads to a new perspective on problems or their resolution.

4-6. Problems typically facing Army forces and unified action partners, within a given area of operations, are human-centered. Human problems are driven by human decision making, which can be affected directly or indirectly through the use of IRCs, including effects produced by movement and maneuver. Therefore, the most essential part of ADM from an IO perspective is framing the current state of the information environment to determine key decision makers and the ways by which their decision process can be altered. This analysis identifies and creates understanding of decision makers' beliefs, motivations, grievances, biases, and preferred ways of communicating and obtaining information.

4-7. Framing the current state and desired future state of the information environment are key aspects of framing an operational environment and developing an operational approach. The operational approach provides a guide for more detailed IO planning, to include determining the effects necessary to bring about the desired end state in the information environment and the required combinations of IRCs needed to produce these effects.

4-8.   Commanders typically employ a combination of direct and indirect approaches to defeating the enemy. A direct approach attacks the threat's center of gravity or principal strength by applying combat power against it. An indirect approach attacks the enemy's center of gravity by applying combat power against a series of decisive points that iteratively lead to the defeat of the center of gravity while avoiding the enemy's strengths. IO contributes to both approaches, especially when the threat's center of gravity or principal strength is information-related. (See ATP 5-0.1, *Army Design Methodology* for a comprehensive discussion of various techniques used in framing the operational environment, framing the problem, developing an operational approach, and reframing).

IO AND THE MILITARY DECISIONMAKING PROCESS

4-9.   Commanders use the MDMP to understand the situation and mission confronting them and make informed decisions resulting in an operations plan or order for execution. (See FM 6-0 for a detailed description of the MDMP.) Their personal interest and involvement is essential to ensuring that IO planning is integrated into MDMP from the beginning and effectively supports mission accomplishment. IO planning is integral to several other processes, to include intelligence preparation of the battlefield (IPB) and targeting. (See ATP 2-01.3 for further information on IPB and Chapter 7 of this manual and ATP 3-60 for further information on targeting.) The G-2 (S-2) and fire support representatives participate in the IO working group and coordinate with the IO officer to integrate IO with their activities and the overall operation. Commanders use their mission statement for the overall operation, the IO mission statement, scheme of IO, IO objectives, and IRC tasks to describe and direct IO, as seen in figure 4-1.

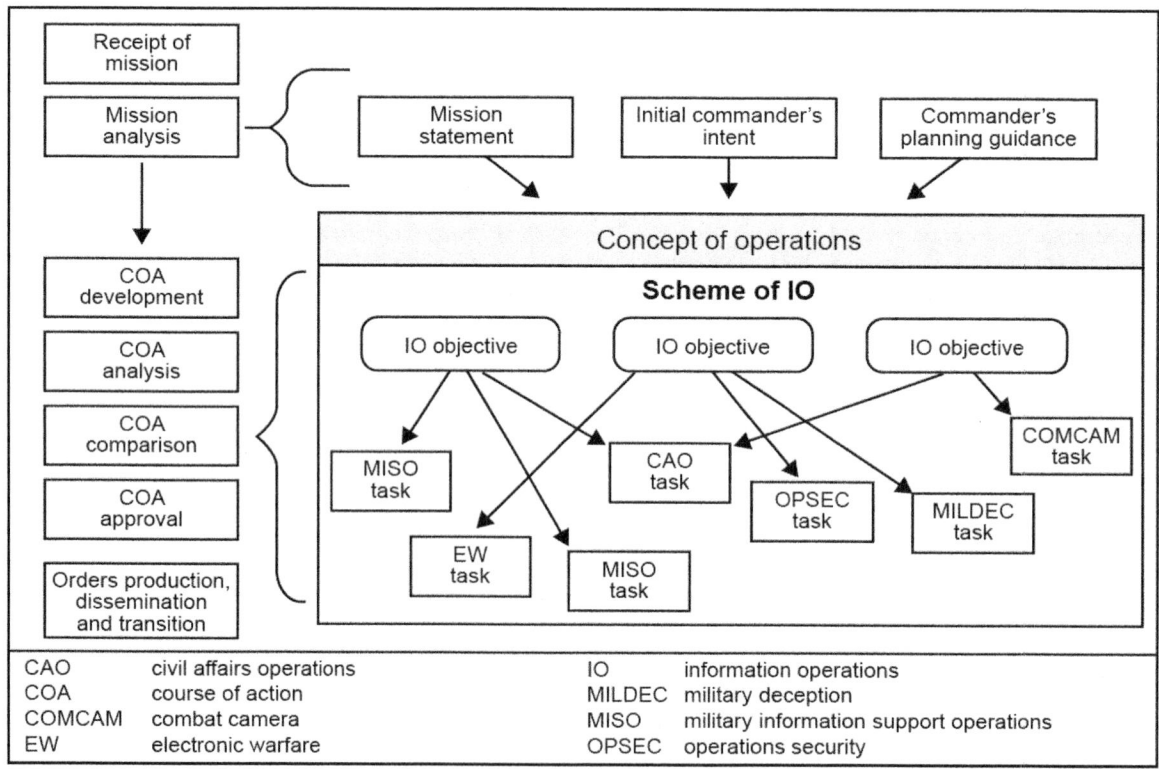

Figure 4-1. Relationship among the scheme of IO, IO objectives, and IRC tasks.

Scheme of IO

4-10.   The scheme of IO is a clear, concise statement of where, when, and how the commander intends to employ and synchronize IRCs, to create effects in and through the information environment to support overall operations and achieve the mission. Based on the commander's planning guidance, to include IO weighted efforts, the IO officer develops a separate scheme of IO for each course of action (COA) the staff develops. IO schemes of support are written in terms of IO objectives—and their associated weighted efforts—and IRC tasks required to achieve these objectives. For example, the overall scheme may be oriented primarily on defending friendly information but also include attack and stabilize objectives.

IO Objectives

4-11. IO objectives express specific and obtainable outcomes or effects that commanders intend to achieve in and through the information environment. In addition to be being specific, these objectives are measurable, achievable, relevant, and time-bounded (or SMART), which facilitates their attainment and assessment (see chapter 8). IO objectives serve a function similar to that of terrain or force-oriented objectives in maneuver operations. They focus the IO effort on achieving synchronized IRC effects, at the right time and place, to accomplish the unit's mission and support the commanders' intent and concept of the operation.

4-12. Accurate situational understanding is key to establishing IO objectives. Operational- and tactical-level IO objectives must nest with strategic theater objectives. Joint and component staffs develop IO objectives to help integrate and synchronize their campaigns and major operations.

4-13. The IO officer develops objectives as part of developing the scheme of IO during COA development. These objectives help the staff determine tasks to subordinate units during COA development and analysis.

Tasks

4-14. Tasks are developed to support accomplishment of one or more IO objectives. These tasks are developed specifically for a given IRC. In concert with IRC representatives, the IO officer develops tasks during COA development and finalizes them during COA analysis. During COA development and COA analysis, tasks are discussed in general terms but not assigned to a subordinate unit. During orders production, these tasks are assigned to IRC units.

Flexibility and Lead Times

4-15. IO planning requires innovation and flexibility. Some IRCs, such as military information support operations (MISO), operations security (OPSEC), and military deception, require a long lead time for planning and preparation. Synchronizing IRCs into multiple lines of operation or effort requires extensive coordination. Achieving certain IO objectives may require senior-leader review and approval and more up-to-date intelligence. For some IRCs, there is a significant lag between execution and assessment of their effects. Planning requires a concentrated information collection effort during preparation and execution to obtain and analyze information for assessing effectiveness. These factors increase the challenges facing planners and decrease the time available to prepare. Nevertheless, early execution of select tasks can enhance efforts to shape the information environment in the area of operations.

RECEIPT OF MISSION

4-16. Upon receipt of a mission, the commander and staff perform an initial assessment. Based on this assessment, the commander issues initial guidance and the staff prepares and issues a warning order (WARNORD). Between receiving the commander's initial guidance and issuing the WARNORD, the staff performs receipt of mission actions. During receipt of mission, the IO officer—

- Reviews and updates the running estimate.
- Participates in the initial assessment.
- Provides input to the commander's initial guidance.
- Provides input to the warning order.
- Prepares for subsequent planning.

REVIEW AND UPDATE THE RUNNING ESTIMATE

4-17. Running estimates are integral to IO planning. A *running estimate* is the continuous assessment of the current situation, and is used to determine if the current operation is proceeding according to the commander's intent and if planned future operations are supportable (ADP 5-0). Running estimates help the IO officer record and track pertinent information about the information environment leading to a basis for recommendations to the commander.

4-18. The IO officer uses the running estimate to assist with completion of each step of the MDMP. An effective running estimate is as comprehensive as possible within the time available but also organized so that the information is easily communicated and processed. Normally, the running estimate provides enough information to draft the applicable IO sections of WARNORDs as required during planning and ultimately to draft applicable IO sections of the operation order (OPORD) or operation plan (OPLAN).

4-19. Variations on the standard, narrative format, such as the example provided in figure 4-2, enable the IO officer to spotlight facts and assumptions, critical planning factors, and available forces. The latter of these requires input from assigned or available IRCs. The graphical format also offers a clear, concise mechanism for the IO officer to articulate recommended high-payoff targets, commander's critical information requirements, and requests for forces. Maintaining both formats simultaneously provides certain benefits: the narrative format enables the IO officer to cut-and-paste sections directly into applicable sections of orders; the graphical format enables the element to brief the commander and staff with a single slide.

4-20. Running estimate development never stops. The IO officer continuously maintains and updates the running estimate as pertinent information is received. While at home station, the IO officer maintains a running estimate on friendly capabilities. If regionally aligned, the unit prepares its estimate based on research and analysis of the information environment within its region and anticipated mission sets.

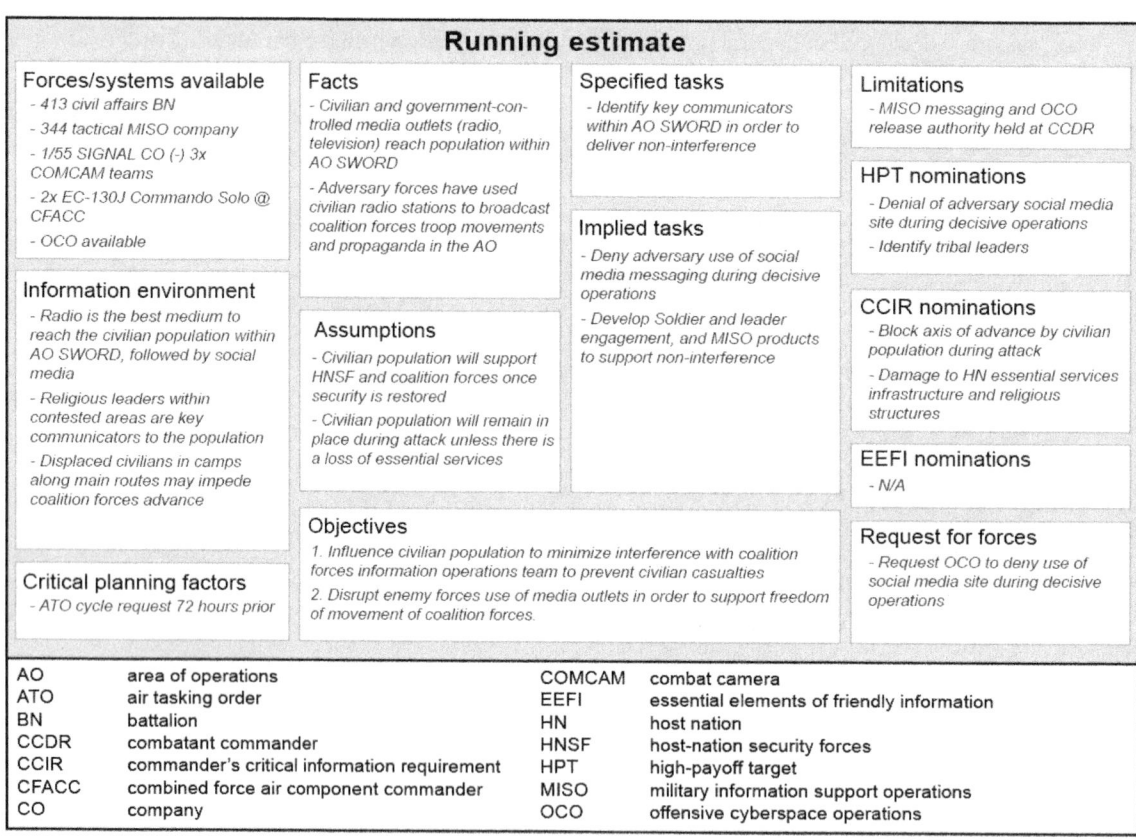

Figure 4-2. Example graphical IO running estimate

PARTICIPATE IN COMMANDER'S INITIAL ASSESSMENT

4-21. Initial assessment primarily focuses on time and resources available to plan, prepare and begin execution of an operation. The IO officer assesses readiness to participate in ADM and MDMP, as well as what external support might be necessary to ensure effective IO planning.

4-22. During the initial assessment, the IO officer establishes a battle rhythm, including locations, times, preparation requirements, and the anticipated schedule. Upon receiving a new mission, the IO officer begins gathering planning tools, including a copy of the higher command OPLAN or OPORD, maps of the area of operations, appropriate references, and the running estimate. During initial assessment, the IO officer also coordinates with organic, assigned, and available IRCs and subordinate units to gauge their planning readiness.

4-23. Initial time allocation is important to IO because some operations and activities require significant time to produce effects or for assessment. The time available may be a limiting factor for some IRCs. The IO officer identifies activities for which this is the case and includes these limitations in estimates and recommendations.

4-24. The commander determines when to execute time-constrained MDMP. Under time-constrained conditions, the IO officer relies on existing tools and products, either his or her own or those of higher headquarters. The lack of time to conduct reconnaissance requires planners to rely more heavily on assumptions and increases the importance of routing combat information and intelligence to the people who need it. A current running estimate is essential to planning in time-constrained conditions.

PROVIDE INPUT TO THE COMMANDER'S INITIAL GUIDANCE

4-25. Commanders include IO-specific guidance in their initial guidance, as required. Examples include authorized movements of IRCs, initiation of information collection necessary to support IO, and delineation of IRs.

PROVIDE INPUT TO THE INITIAL WARNING ORDER

4-26. A WARNORD is issued after the commander and staff have completed their initial assessment and before mission analysis begins. It includes, at a minimum, the type and general location of the operation, initial timeline, and any movements or reconnaissance that need to be initiated. When they receive the initial WARNORD, subordinate units begin parallel planning.

4-27. Parallel planning and collaborative planning are routine MDMP techniques. The time needed to achieve and assess effects in the information environment makes it especially important to successful IO. Effective parallel or collaborative planning requires all echelons to share information fully as soon as it is available. Information sharing includes providing higher headquarters plans, orders, and guidance to subordinate IO officers or representatives.

4-28. Because some IRCs require a long time to plan or must begin execution early in an operation, follow-on WARNORDs may include detailed IO information. Although the MDMP includes three points at which commanders issue WARNORDs, the number of WARNORDs is not fixed. WARNORDs serve a purpose in planning similar to that of a fragmentary order (FRAGORD) during execution. Commanders issue both, as the situation requires. Possible IO officer input to the initial WARNORD includes:

- Tasks to subordinate units and IRCs for early initiation of approved IO actions, particularly for military deception operations and MISO.
- Essential elements of friendly information (EEFIs) to facilitate defend weighted efforts and begin the OPSEC process.
- Known hazards and risk guidance.
- Military deception guidance and priorities.

MISSION ANALYSIS

4-29. Commanders and their staff conduct mission analysis to better understand the situation and problem, and to identify the purpose of the operation. It is the most important step in MDMP and consists of 18 sub-steps, many of which are performed concurrently. (See FM 6-0, Chapter 9) The IO officer ensures each output or product from this step includes relevant factors or tie-ins. The IO officer also participates in other staff processes (such as IPB and targeting) to ensure IO is properly integrated. For the IO officer, mission analysis focuses on developing information and products that will be used during the rest of the operations process.

ANALYZE HIGHER HEADQUARTERS' PLAN OR ORDER

4-30. Mission analysis begins with a thorough examination of the higher headquarters OPLAN/OPORD in terms of the commander's initial guidance. By examining higher echelon plans, commanders and staffs learn how higher headquarters plan to conduct IO and which resources and higher headquarters assets are available. The IO officer researches these plans and orders to understand the—

- Higher commander's intent and concept of operations.
- Higher headquarters area of operations and interest, mission and task constraints, acceptable risk, and available assets.
- Higher headquarters schedule for conducting the operation.
- Missions of adjacent units.

4-31. Planning to conduct IO without considering these factors may result in an uncoordinated operation, which will hamper overall mission effectiveness. A thorough analysis also helps to determine if additional, external IO support is necessary.

PERFORM INITIAL INTELLIGENCE PREPARATION OF THE BATTLEFIELD

4-32. During mission analysis, the G-2 (S-2) prepares IPB products or updates existing products and the initial IPB is performed upon receipt of the mission. The G-2 (S-2), with assistance and input from other staff elements, uses IPB to define the area of operations/interest, describe its effects, evaluate the threat, and determine threat courses of action. Figure 4-3, on page 4-8, lists possible IO-related factors to consider during each IPB step. During IPB, the IO officer works with the G-2 (S-2) to determine threat capabilities and vulnerabilities in the information environment regarding both the threat and other relevant targets and audiences in the area of operations.

Define the Information Environment

4-33. The information environment has always affected military operations. IO officers, working with the G-2 (S-2), use available intelligence to analyze the information environment and the threat's use of information. This information is submitted to the G-2 (S-2) to answer intelligence gaps that address how information environment factors affect operations. The G-2 (S-2) obtains the information from strategic and national-level databases, country studies, collection assets and, when necessary, other intelligence agencies.

4-34. As part of defining the battlefield environment, the G-2 (S-2) establishes the limits of the area of interest. The area of interest includes areas outside the area of operations that are occupied by threat or other forces/groups that can affect mission accomplishment. This fact is particularly true from an information environment perspective. The ability to obtain and pass information has vastly expanded the capacity of actors to affect areas of operations from anywhere. The IO officer ensures that the G-2 (S-2) considers this factor of the information environment in defining the area of interest for IPB.

4-35. As stated in Chapter 2, one of the enabling activities of IO is analyzing and understanding the information environment in all its complexity. Using the IPB process to accomplish this task, the IO officer develops a series of information overlays, as well as combined information overlays, to depict the information aspects of the operational environment.

4-36. The IO officer provides input to help the G-2 (S-2) develop IPB templates, databases, social network diagrams, and other products that portray information about threats and other key groups or audiences in the areas of operation and interest. These products contain information about each group's leaders and decision makers. Information relevant to conducting IO includes, but is not limited to:

- Religion, language, culture, and internet activities of key groups and decision makers.
- Agendas of non-governmental organizations.
- Military and civilian communication infrastructures and connectivity.
- Population demographics, linkages, and related information.
- Location and types of radars, jammers, and other non-communication information systems.
- Audio, video, and print media outlets and centers; the populations they serve; and their dissemination characteristics, such as frequency, range, language, etc.
- Command and control or mission command vulnerabilities of friendly, adversary, and other forces or groups.
- Conduit analysis describing how threat decision makers receive information.

4-37. Threat templates portray how adversaries use forces and assets unopposed by friendly forces and capabilities. Threat templates are often developed before deployment. The G-2 (S-2) and IO officer may add factors from the information environment to a maneuver-based threat template, or they may prepare a separate IO threat template. The situation, available information, and type of threat affect the approach taken. IO-related portions of IPB products become part of paragraph 1b of the running estimate.

4-38. The G-2 (S-2) uses IPB to determine possible threat courses of action and arrange them in probable order of adoption. These courses of action, depicted as situation templates, include threat IRCs. A comprehensive IPB addresses threat offensive and defensive capabilities and vulnerabilities, and it is efficacious to friendly mission analysis to develop situation templates depicting how threats and others may employ these capabilities to achieve advantage.

IPB Support of Targeting

4-39. IPB identifies high-value targets (HVTs) and shows where and when they may be anticipated. Some of these HVTs are IO-focused or related, such as a specific population group within an area of operation. The G-2 (S-2) works with the IO officer to develop IO-related HVTs into high-payoff targets (HPTs) for the commander's approval. The IO officer determines which HPTs are related to one or more objectives and develops tasks to engage those targets during COA development and analysis.

Other IPB Products

4-40. IPB identifies facts and assumptions concerning threats and the operational environment that the IO officer considers during planning. These are incorporated into paragraph 2 of the running estimate. The IO officer submits IRs to update facts and verify assumptions. Working with the G-2 (S-2) and other staff sections, the IO officer ensures IRs are clearly identified and requests for information (RFIs) are submitted to the appropriate agency when necessary. IPB may create priority intelligence requirements (PIRs) pertinent to IO planning. The IO officer may nominate these as commander's critical information requirements (CCIRs) and also identify OPSEC vulnerabilities. The IO officer analyzes these to determine appropriate OPSEC measures.

Define the Operational Environment	Describe the Environmental Effects on Operations	Evaluate the Threat	Determine Threat COAs
Portions or aspects of the information environment that can effect friendly operations. Features/activities that can influence information and threat command and control (C2) or friendly mission command systems. Political and governmental structures and population demographics. Major cultures, languages, religions, and ethnic groups. Civilian communication and power infrastructures (both physical and informational). Non-state actors, non-governmental organizations and significant non-threat groups. Types of and public access to media or press outlets.	IE effects on decisionmakers, C2 or mission command systems, and decision-making processes. How the IE relates to the area of operations. IE effects on friendly, threat, and other operations. Combined effects of friendly, threat, and other information, and C2 or mission command systems on the information environment. Effects of terrain, weather, and other characteristics of the area of operations on friendly and enemy information and C2 or mission command systems. Effect of public media or press on friendly and threat operations.	Adversary and other group C2 systems, including functions, assets, capabilities, and vulnerabilities (both offensive and defensive). Assets and functions (such as decisionmakers, C2 systems, and decision-making processes) that adversaries and others require to operate effectively. Adversary capabilities to attack friendly information systems and defend their own. Models of threat and other group C2 systems. IO or information-related strength, vulnerabilities, and susceptibilities of adversaries and other groups.	How threats and other groups pursue operational or decisive advantage in the IE. How, when, where, and why (to what purpose) threats and other groups will use information-related capabilities to achieve their likely objectives.
C2 command and control	**COA** Course of Action	**IE** Information environment	**IO** Information operations

Figure 4-3. IO-related factors to consider during IPB

DETERMINE SPECIFIED, IMPLIED, AND ESSENTIAL TASKS

4-41. While the staff determines specified, implied, and essential tasks the unit must perform, the IO officer identifies specified IO tasks in the higher headquarters OPLAN or OPORD. The IO officer also develops IO-related implied tasks that support accomplishing identified specified tasks. These identified tasks are the basis of the initial scheme of IO developed during COA development.

IO officers look for specified tasks that may involve IO in the higher headquarters OPLAN or OPORD, paying particular attention to:

- Paragraph 1, Situation.
- Paragraph 2, Mission.
- Paragraph 3, Execution, especially subparagraphs on IO, tasks to subordinate units, and CCIRs.
- Annexes and appendices that address intelligence, operations, fire support, rules of engagement, IO, IRCs, information collection, assessment, and interagency coordination.

4-42. Some IO specified tasks, such as support to the higher headquarters deception plan, become unit objectives. Others, particularly those that address only one IRC, are incorporated under IO objectives as tasks. As the staff identifies specified tasks for the overall operation, the IO officer deduces the steps that are necessary to accomplish these specified tasks. These tasks become IO implied tasks. Once the IO officer identifies specified and implied tasks and understands each task's requirements and purpose, essential tasks are identified. An essential task is a specified or implied task that must be executed to accomplish the mission. If the command must accomplish an IO task to accomplish its mission, that task is an essential task for the command and is included in the recommended mission statement.

REVIEW AVAILABLE ASSETS AND IDENTIFY RESOURCE SHORTFALLS

4-43. During this sub-step, the commander and staff determine if they have the assets required to perform the specified, implied, and essential tasks. The IO officer performs this analysis to determine if the requisite capabilities are on hand or available through coordination with higher echelons to achieve the effects in the information environment necessary to support the mission. At echelons below division, units have few organic IRCs other than movement and maneuver; Soldier and leader engagement; and presence, posture, and profile. If additional IRCs are required, the IO officer works with the operations officer to request these capabilities and ensure appropriate authorities exist. (See chapter 9 for further discussion of IO at brigade and below).

4-44. The IO officer compares available IRCs with the tasks that need to be accomplished to identify capability shortfalls and additional resources required. The IO officer considers how the following will affect attainment of IO objectives and whether additional capacity is required—

- Changes in task organization.
- Limitations of available units and IRCs.
- Nature of effects that need to be achieved in the information environment and the tasks to accomplish them.
- The need for redundancy or repetition to achieve desired effects.
- The level, quantity, and quality of expertise on hand.

DETERMINE CONSTRAINTS

4-45. A constraint is a restriction placed on the command by a higher command. A constraint dictates an action or inaction, thus restricting the freedom of action of a subordinate commander (FM 6-0). IO constraints include legal, moral, social, operational, and political factors. They also include limitations imposed by various authorities, such as the Secretary of Defense or U.S. ambassador. Constraints may be listed in the following paragraphs, annexes or appendices of the higher OPLAN/OPORD—

- Commander's intent and guidance.
- Tasks to subordinate units.
- Rules of engagement (no strike list, restricted target list)
- Civil affairs operations.
- MISO
- Fire support.

4-46. Constraints establish limits within which the commander can conduct IO. Constraints may also limit the use of military deception and some OPSEC measures. One output of this sub-step is a list of the constraints that the IO officer believes will affect the scheme of IO.

IDENTIFY CRITICAL FACTS AND DEVELOP ASSUMPTIONS

4-47. Sources of facts and assumptions include existing plans, initial guidance, observations, and reports. Some facts concerning friendly forces are determined during the review of the available assets. During IPB, the G-2 (S-2), with assistance from the IO officer and other staff elements, develops facts and assumptions about threats and others, the area of operations, and the information environment. The following categories of information are important to the IO officer—

- Intelligence on threat commanders and other key leaders.
- Threat morale.
- Media and/or press coverage of threat and other relevant audiences in the area of operations.
- The weather.
- Dispositions of adversary, friendly, and other key groups.
- Available troops, unit strengths, and materiel readiness.
- Friendly force IO vulnerabilities.
- Threat and other key group IO vulnerabilities.

4-48. The primary output of this sub-step is a list of facts and assumptions that concern IO. These are placed in paragraph 1c of the running estimate. The IO officer prepares and submits to appropriate agencies IO IRs for information that would confirm or disprove facts and assumptions. The IO officer reviews facts and assumptions as information is received and revises facts or converts assumptions into facts.

BEGIN RISK MANAGEMENT

4-49. Commanders and staffs assess risk when they identify hazards, regardless of type. The IO officer assesses IO-associated risk throughout the operations process. The G-3 (S-3) incorporates the IO risk assessment into the command's overall risk assessment.

4-50. IO-related hazards fall into three categories:

- OPSEC vulnerabilities, including hazards associated with compromise of essential elements of friendly information.
- Mission command vulnerabilities, including those associated with the loss of critical assets or identified during the vulnerability assessment.
- Hazards associated with executing IO tasks.

4-51. During mission analysis, the IO officer assesses primarily OPSEC- and mission command-related hazards, as well as hazards associated with IO-related specified and implied tasks identified up to this point in mission analysis. The list of task-associated hazards is refined during COA development, after articulating IRC tasks that support IO objectives. The IO element uses experience in previous operations as a means of identifying known or expected hazards, and IRC representatives often best articulate hazards associated with their tasks.

4-52. As with all operations, IO entails risk. Resource constraints, combined with threat reactions and initiatives, reduce the degree and scope of advantage possible in the information environment. Risk assessment is one means commanders use to allocate resources. Staffs identify which hazards pose the greatest threat to mission accomplishment. They then determine the resources required to control them and estimate the benefits gained. This estimate of residual risk gives commanders a tool to help decide how to allocate resources and where to accept risk. (For detailed information on the integration of the risk management process, see ATP 5-19).

DEVELOP COMMANDER'S CRITICAL INFORMATION REQUIREMENTS AND ESSENTIAL ELEMENTS OF FRIENDLY INFORMATION

4-53. A *commander's critical information requirement* (CCIR) is an information requirement identified by the commander as being critical to facilitating timely decision making (JP 3-0). CCIRs include priority intelligence requirements (PIRs) and friendly forces information requirements (FFIRs). Staff sections, including the IO officer, recommend CCIRs to the G-3 (S-3). In a time-constrained environment, the staff may collectively compile this information. The G-3 (S-3) presents a consolidated list of CCIRs to the commander for approval. The commander determines the final CCIRs.

4-54. Establishing CCIRs is one means commanders use to focus assessment efforts. CCIRs change throughout the operations process because the information that affects decision making changes as an operation progresses.

4-55. During planning, staff sections establish IRs to obtain the information they need to develop the plan. Commanders produce CCIRs to support decisions they must make regarding the form the plan takes.

4-56. During preparation, the focus of IRs and CCIRs shifts to decisions required to refine the plan. During execution, commanders establish CCIRs that identify the information they need to make execution and adjustment decisions.

4-57. During mission analysis, the IO officer derives the information needed by the commander to determine how to employ IO during the upcoming operation. The IO officer recommends the IO IRs to be included in the CCIRs. This sub-step produces no IO-specific product unless the IO officer recommends one or more IO IRs as CCIRs. However, at this point, the IO officer should have assembled a list of IO IRs and submitted friendly-force-related IRs to the G-3 (S-3) and threat-related IRs to the G-2 (S-2).

4-58. The following is an example of CCIRs for a stability operation in which an information operation is the decisive operation:

- Who are the municipality's key players in ethnic violence?
- What are the interests of the political parties?

- Who are the formal and informal leaders within the political parties?
- How can friendly forces exploit political party interests to garner support?
- Which party represents the majority of the people, but also actively support progress within the municipality?
- What is the status of IRCs within the area of operations?

4-59. In addition to nominating CCIRs to the commander, the staff also identifies and nominates essential elements of friendly information, or EEFIs. EEFIs are elements of information to protect rather than to collect, and identify those elements of friendly force information that, if compromised, would jeopardize mission success. Although EEFIs are not CCIRs, they have the same priority as CCIRs and require approval by the commander. Like CCIRs, EEFIs change as an operation progresses (FM 6-0).

4-60. Submission of IO-focused requirements for potential inclusion as CCIRs, along with other CCIRs, enable the staff to develop the initial information collection plan. Approval of EEFIs enable the staff to plan and implement friendly force information protection measures, such as provided by military deception and OPSEC.

DEVELOP THE INITIAL INFORMATION COLLECTION PLAN

4-61. The staff identifies information gaps, especially those needed to answer IRs. The IO officer identifies gaps in information needed to support IO planning, execution and assessment. These are submitted to the G-2 (S-2) as IO IRs. The initial information collection plan sets the priorities for information collection in order to answer CCIRs. The G-3 (S-3) issues the information collection plan as part of a WARNORD, a FRAGORD or an OPORD. Within these orders, the information collection plan is found in Annex L.

UPDATE PLAN FOR THE USE OF AVAILABLE TIME

4-62. At this point, the G-3 (S-3) refines the initial time plan developed during receipt of mission. The IO officer provides input specifying the long lead-time items associated with certain IRC tasks (such as military deception and MISO). Upon receiving the revised timeline, the IO officer compares the time available to accomplish IRC tasks with the command's and threat's time lines, and revises the IO time allocation plan accordingly. The IO product for this sub-step is a revised time plan.

DEVELOP INITIAL THEMES AND MESSAGES

4-63. Gaining and maintaining the trust of relevant audiences and actors is an important aspect of operations. Faced with a diverse array of individuals, organizations, and publics who affect or are affected by their unit's operations, commanders identify and engage entities vital to operational success. The behaviors of these entities can aid or complicate the friendly forces' challenges as commanders strive to accomplish missions.

4-64. The IO officer does not develop themes and messages. This is done by the public affairs officer and MISO element. The public affairs officer adjusts and refines themes and messages received from higher headquarters for use by the command. These themes and messages are designed to inform specific domestic and foreign audiences about current or planned military operations. The Office of the Secretary of Defense, Department of State, or geographic combatant commander (depending on the operation) provides applicable themes to MISO forces, which then develop actions and messages. The highest level MISO element in theater adjusts or refines the themes depending on the situation. It employs themes and messages as part of planned activities designed to influence specific foreign targets and audiences for various purposes that support current or planned operations.

4-65. The commander and the chief of staff approve all themes and messages used to support operations in their area of responsibility. Although the IO officer does not develop themes and messages, they do assist the G-3 (S-3) and the commander to de-conflict and synchronize IRCs used specifically to execute actions for psychological effect and deliver messages during operations.

DEVELOP A PROPOSED PROBLEM STATEMENT

4-66. Problem statements are typically developed during design. If this did not occur prior to mission analysis, it is accomplished during this step of the MDMP. If done during design, the commander and staff revise the problem statement based on their enhanced understanding of the situation. The key is identifying the right problem to solve, because it leads to the formulation of specific solution-sets. In identifying the problem, the commander and staff compare the current situation to the desired end state and list issues that impede the unit from achieving this end state.

4-67. Given the increasing impact of the information environment, the prevailing problem or impeding issues are likely to be information-related. Also, information-related problems can be more complex and multi-dimensional than geographical or technological problems or impediments. Therefore, it is essential to spend the time necessary to articulate the problem and impediments as carefully and clearly as possible.

DEVELOP A PROPOSED MISSION STATEMENT

4-68. The G-3 (S-3) or executive officer develops the proposed restated mission based on the force's essential tasks, which the commander approves or modifies. The IO officer provides input based on the current IO running estimate. The mission statement includes any identified IO essential tasks.

4-69. Mission statements should use tactical mission tasks, which are specific activities performed by units while executing a form of tactical operation or form of maneuver (See ATP 3-90.1). IO tasks do not always neatly fit into this framework, as they are rarely terrain- or combined arms-based. However, if they are framed in terms of friendly force actions (for example, influence the population in a certain area) or effects on threat forces (deceive the threat's reserve forces commander), and if they support the commander's intent and planning guidance, then they can be integrated effectively into the restated mission.

4-70. The IO officer also develops an IO mission statement that guides IO execution and ensures IO objectives are accomplished. The IO mission statement is explicitly stated in Appendix 15 (Information Operations) to Annex C (Operations) of the base order. (See FM 6-0, Appendix C, for additional details on functional area mission statements.)

PRESENT THE MISSION ANALYSIS BRIEFING

4-71. The staff briefs the commander on the results of its mission analysis. The mission analysis briefing is an essential means for the commander, staff, subordinates and other partners to develop a shared understanding of the upcoming operation and the interrelationships among the mission variables and elements of combat power. IO input is based on its running estimate, analysis in the foregoing steps, and how IO impacts or is impacted by other areas and functions. Time permitting, the staff employs the outline provided in figure 4-4.

DEVELOP AND ISSUE INITIAL COMMANDER'S INTENT

4-72. The *commander's intent* is a clear and concise expression of the purpose of the operation and the desired military end state that supports mission command, provides focus to the staff, and helps subordinate and supporting commanders act to achieve the commander's desired results without further orders, even when the operation does not unfold as planned (JP 3-0). The IO officer develops recommended input to the commander's intent and submits it to the G-3 (S-3) for the commander's consideration. When developing recommended input to the commander's intent, the IO officer assists the commander in visualizing and understanding the information environment, ways it will affect operations, and ways that IO can affect the information environment to the commander's advantage.

DEVELOP AND ISSUE INITIAL PLANNING GUIDANCE

4-73. After approving the restated mission and issuing the intent, commanders provide additional guidance to focus staff planning activities. As appropriate, the commander includes their visualization of IO in this guidance. Commanders consider the following when developing their IO planning guidance:
- Aspects of higher headquarters IO policies or guidance that the commander wants to emphasize.

- Aspects of the mission for which IO is most likely to increase the chance of success or which may be IO-dominant.
- Risks they are willing to take with respect to IO.
- IO decisions for which they want to retain or delegate authority.

Outline	Information Operations Input
Mission and commander's intent of headquarters two echelons up.	IO specified and implied tasks
Mission commander's intent, concept of operations of headquarters one echelon up.	IO specified and implied tasks
Proposed problem statement	Information-related problems within the IE.
Proposed mission statement	IO essential tasks
Review of commander's initial guidance	• Guidance concerning IO • EEFI and CCIR • Essential narrative elements
Initial IPB products	Information overlays
Specified, implied, and essential tasks	Specified, implied, and essential tasks for IO
Constraints	Any constraints placed on the command affecting IO
Initial risk assessment	• Recommended OPSEC planning guidance • Recommended controls to protect information-related vulnerabilities and critical assets. • Recommended controls for risk associated with IO tasks
Proposed themes and messages	Possible overlaps or conflicts among IRCs used to disseminate approved themes and messages.
Proposed timeline	• Time required to accomplish IO • Analysis of time needed versus time available

CCIR Commander's Critical Information Requirements	EEFI Essential element of friendly information	IO Information Operations	IPB Intelligence preparation of the battlefield

Figure 4-4. Information operations input to mission analysis briefing

4-74. Planning guidance focuses on the command's essential tasks. Commanders may give guidance for IO separately or as part of their overall guidance. This guidance includes any identified or contemplated IO objectives, stated in finite and measurable terms. It may also include OPSEC planning guidance, military deception guidance, and targeting guidance.

4-75. Factors that the IO officer considers when recommending input to initial planning guidance include:
- The extent that the command is vulnerable to hostile information-based warfare.
- Specific IO actions required for the operation.
- The command's capability to execute specific actions or weighted efforts.
- Additional information needed to conduct IO.

DEVELOP COURSE OF ACTION EVALUATION CRITERIA

4-76. Course of action (COA) evaluation criteria are used during course of action analysis and comparison to measure the relative effectiveness and efficiency of COAs to another. They are developed during this sub-step to enhance objectivity and lessen the chances of bias. Typically, the chief of staff will develop the criterion and associated weight. The IO officer will propose possible refinement to ensure consideration of IO factors affecting success or failure and then employ approved criteria to score each COA.

ISSUE WARNING ORDER

4-77. As the mission and operation dictate, the WARNORD will include essential IO tasks within the mission statement. It will note changes to task organization involving IRC or IO units and address IO factors in other relevant paragraphs, sections, or annexes, as appropriate.

4-78. Table 4-1 provides a summary of the inputs, actions and outputs required of the IO officer. Only those sub-steps within mission analysis with significant IO activity are listed.

Table 4-1. Mission Analysis

MDMP Sub-Step	Inputs	IO Officer Actions	IO Officer Outputs
Conduct IPB	• Higher HQ IPB • Higher HQ running estimates • Higher HQ OPLAN or OPORD • Higher HQ combined information overlay	• Develop IPB products • Analyze and describe the information environment in the unit's area of operations and its effect on friendly, neutral, adversary, and enemy information efforts • Identify threat information capabilities and vulnerabilities • Identify gaps in current intelligence on threat information efforts • Identify IO-related high-value targets • Determine probable threat information-related COAs • Assess the potential effects of IO on friendly, neutral, adversary, and enemy operations • Determine threat's ability to collect on friendly critical information • Determine additional EEFIs (OPSEC)	• Input to IPB products • IRs to G-2 (S-2), as well as the foreign disclosure officer • Refined EEFIs (OPSEC)

Table 4.1. Mission Analysis (continued)

MDMP Sub-Step	Inputs	IO Officer Actions	IO Officer Outputs
Determine Specified, Implied, and Essential Tasks	• Specified tasks from higher HQ OPLAN or OPORD • IPB and combined information overlay products	• Identify specified tasks in the higher HQ OPLAN or OPORD • Develop implied tasks • Determine if there are any essential tasks • Develop input to the command targeting guidance • Assemble critical and defended asset lists, especially low density delivery systems • Determine additional EEFIs (OPSEC)	• Specified, implied and essential tasks • List of IRCs to G-3 (S-3) • Input to command targeting guidance • Refined EEFIs (OPSEC)
Review Available Assets	• Current task organization for information related capabilities • Higher HQ task organization for information related capabilities • Status reports • Unit standard operating procedure	• Identify friendly IRCs (include capabilities that are joint, interorganizational, and multinational) • Analyze IRC command and support relationships • Determine if available IRCs can perform tasks necessary to support lines of operation or effort • Identify additional resources (such as air assets) needed to execute or support IO	• List of available IRCs [IO running estimate paragraph 1b(4)] • Request for additional IRCs, if required
Determine Constraints	• Commander's initial guidance • Higher HQ OPLAN or OPORD	• Identify IO-related constraints	• List of constraints (IO appendix to Annex C; scheme of IO or coordinating instructions)
Identify Critical Facts and Develop Assumptions	• Higher HQ OPLAN or OPORD • Commander's initial guidance • Observations and reports	• Identify facts and assumptions affecting IRCs • Submit IRs that will confirm or disprove assumptions • Identify facts and assumptions regarding OPSEC indicators that identify vulnerabilities	• List of facts and assumptions (IO running estimate paragraph 1c.) • IRs that will confirm or disprove facts and assumptions

Table 4.1. Mission Analysis (continued)

MDMP Sub-Step	Inputs	IO Officer Actions	IO Officer Outputs
Begin Risk Management	• Higher HQ OPLAN or OPORD • IPB • Commander's initial guidance	• Identify and assess hazards associated with IO • Propose controls • Identify OPSEC indicators • Assess risk associated with OPSEC indicators to determine vulnerabilities • Establish OPSEC measures	• List of assessed hazards • Input to risk assessment • Develop risk briefing matrix • List of provisional OPSEC measures
Develop Initial CCIRs and EEFIs	• IO IRs	• Determine information the commander needs in order to make critical decisions concerning IO efforts • Identify IRs to recommend as commander's critical information requirements	• Submit IRs
Determine Initial Information Collection Plan	• Initial IPB • PIRs or IO IRs	• Identify gaps in information needed to support planning, execution, and assessment of early initiation actions • Confirm that the initial information collection plan includes IRs concerning enemy capability to collect EEFIs	
Update Plan for the Use of Available Time	• Revised G-5 (S-5)/G-3 (S-3) plans timeline	• Determine time to accomplish IO planning requirements • Assess viability of planning timeline vis-à-vis higher HQ timeline and threat timeline as determined during IPB • Refine initial time allocation plan	• Timeline (provided to G-5 (S-5), with emphasis on the effect(s) of long-lead time events
Develop Initial Themes and Messages	• Public affairs themes and messages adjusted and refined from higher HQ • MISO actions and messages adjusted and refined from higher HQ	• Assess impact of initial themes and messages on the information environment • Assess whether planned IO effects will reinforce themes and messages • Contribute to development of talking points aimed at influencing perceptions and behaviors	• PA themes/ messages and MISO actions/ messages de-conflicted • Initial list of talking points • IRC actions to disseminate approved messages/ talking points

Table 4.1. Mission Analysis (continued)

MDMP Sub-Step	Inputs	IO Officer Actions	IO Officer Outputs
Develop Proposed Problem Statement and Mission Statement	• Initial IO mission • Initial IO objectives • Approved themes and messages	• List issues and determine primary obstacles that impede achieving the desired end state in the information environment • Recommend possible initial objectives for inclusion in the restated mission	• Input to proposed problem statement • Essential tasks • Restated mission • Revised or additional initial objectives recommended for inclusion in the restated mission • Updated synchronization of themes and messages with actions
Present Mission Analysis Briefing	• IO running estimate. • Unit standard operating procedure	• Prepare to brief IO portion of mission analysis	• IO portion of mission analysis briefing
Develop and Issue Initial Commander's Intent	• Higher HQ commander's intent • Results of mission analysis • IO running estimate	• Develop recommended input to the commander's intent and narrative	• Recommend input to the commander's intent and narrative
Develop and Issue Initial Planning Guidance	• Higher HQ OPLAN or OPORD • Results of mission analysis • IO running estimate	• Develop recommended input to the commander's guidance • Combine the refined EEFIs with the provisional OPSEC measures to produce the planning guidance	• Recommended input to the commander's guidance • Recommended OPSEC planning guidance • Recommended military deception guidance, to include guidance on using deception in support of OPSEC, if appropriate • Recommended IO targeting guidance

Table 4.1. Mission Analysis (continued)

MDMP Sub-Step	Inputs	IO Officer Actions	IO Officer Outputs

Issue a Warning Order	• Commander's intent and guidance
	• Approved restated mission and initial objectives
	• Mission analysis products
		• Prepare input to the warning order. Input may include —
		  – Early tasking to subordinate units
		  – Initial mission statement
		  – OPSEC planning guidance
		  – Reconnaissance and surveillance tasking
		• Military deception guidance
			• Input to mission, commander's intent, commander's critical information requirements, and concept of the operations

COA course of action **EEFI** essential element of friendly information **G-2** assistant chief of staff, intelligence **G-3** assistant chief of staff, operations **G-5** assistant chief of staff, plans **HQ** headquarters **IO** information operations	**IPB** intelligence preparation of the battlefield **IR** information requirements **IRC** information related capability **MISO** military information support operations **OPLAN** operations plan **OPORD** operations order	**OPSEC** operations security **PA** public affairs **PIR** priority intelligence requirement **S-2** battalion or brigade intelligence officer **S-3** battalion or brigade operations staff officer **S-5** battalion or brigade plans staff officer	

COURSE OF ACTION DEVELOPMENT

4-79. After the mission analysis briefing, the staff begins developing COAs for analysis and comparison based on the restated mission, commander's intent, and planning guidance. During COA development, the staff prepares feasible COAs that integrate the effects of all combat power elements to accomplish the mission. Based on the unit's approved mission statement, the IO officer develops a distinct scheme of IO, IO objectives, and IRC tasks for each COA.

4-80. The IO officer is involved early in COA development. The focus is on determining how to achieve decisive advantage in and through the information environment at the critical times and places of each COA. Depending on the time available, planning products may be written or verbal.

ASSESS RELATIVE COMBAT POWER

4-81. IO synchronization of IRCs enhances the combat power, constructive and destructive, of friendly forces in numerous ways. Some examples include:

- Military deception influences application (or misapplication) of threat forces and capabilities at places and times that favor friendly operations.
- Countering the effects of propaganda degrades threat propaganda efforts by exposing lies and providing accurate information.
- MISO and civil military operations favorably influence foreign audiences by emphasizing the positive actions of U.S. forces.
- Movement and maneuver destroys or disrupts threat communicators, controls territory through which information flows, and influences affected populations.
- Electronic warfare jams threat communications and command and control signals.
- Fires destroys threat communication infrastructure.

4-82. The IO officer ensures that the staff considers IO when analyzing relative combat power. IO can be especially valuable in reducing resource expenditures by other combat power elements. For example, commanders can use electronic warfare to jam a communications node instead of using fires to destroy it.

4-83. IO contributions are often difficult to factor into numerical force ratios. With IO officer support, staff planners consider the effects of IO on the intangible factors of military operations as they assess relative combat power. Intangible factors include such things as the uncertainty of war and the will of friendly forces and the threat. Varied approaches and methods may be used to achieve IO effects. One method is to increase the relative combat power assigned to forces who effectively employ organic IRCs. For example, strict OPSEC discipline by friendly forces increases the difficulty the threat has in collecting information. Units with a Theater IO Group OPSEC support detachment may further increase their relative combat power as a result of this augmentation.

GENERATE OPTIONS

4-84. Options are expressed as COAs. Given the increasing impact of the information environment on operations and the threat's use of information-focused warfare to gain advantage, staffs recognize that, in certain COAs, IO may be the main effort.

4-85. The IO officer assists the staff in considering the ways that IO can support each COA. This requires the IO officer to determine which IRCs to employ and the trade-offs associated with each. In brainstorming options, the IO officer thinks first in an unconstrained manner, then refines available options based on the running estimate and knowledge of available assets and those that are anticipated. During this sub-step, the IO officer also develops input to military deception COAs, if applicable. The main output of this effort is an initial scheme of IO by phase for each COA.

ARRAY FORCES

4-86. The staff arrays forces to determine the forces necessary to accomplish the mission and to develop a knowledge base for making decisions concerning concepts of operations. The IO officer ensures planners consider the impact of available IRCs on force ratios as they determine the initial placements. IRCs may reduce the number of maneuver forces required or may increase the COA options available. Planners consider the deception story during this step because aspects of it may affect unit positioning.

4-87. Although the staff considered IRC availability when developing COAs, this step allows them to further validate if the required capabilities are present and, if not, determine if they can be obtained and positioned in time to achieve required effects. It also enables the IO officer to determine if available IRCs are properly positioned and task-organized.

DEVELOP A BROAD CONCEPT

4-88. The broad concept concisely expresses the "how" of the commander's visualization and will eventually provide the framework for the concept of operations and summarizes the contributions of all warfighting functions (FM 6-0). The IO officer develops schemes of IO and IO objectives for each COA that nest with the broad concept. With input from IRC representatives, the IO officer considers how IRCs can achieve the IO objectives.

4-89. IO schemes of support are further expressed in terms of the weighted efforts required to support the overall concept of operations. Depending on proportion of offense, defense, and stability tasks, the IO officer determines the best mix of attack, defend, and stability IO efforts needed to ensure achievement of objectives. The IO officer then determines which IRCs to allocate to each effort and possible tasking conflicts.

4-90. During this sub-step, the IO officer develops control measures, critical and defended asset lists, and additional EEFIs for each COA, as well as determines OPSEC vulnerabilities and measures. Most importantly, the IO officer produces five essential, often time-intensive, outputs. These are—

- COA worksheets.
- Synchronization matrix.
- Target nominations.

- Risk assessment.
- Measures of performance and effectiveness.

COA Worksheets

4-91. The IO officer employs COA worksheets to prepare for COA analysis and focus IRC efforts. These worksheets can be narrative or graphical or a combination of both. The IO officer prepares one worksheet for each IO objective in each scheme of IO. IO worksheets include the following information, as a minimum:

- A description of the COA.
- The scheme of IO in statement form.
- The IO objective in statement form.
- Information concerning IRC tasks that support the objective, listed by IRC.
- Anticipated adversary counteractions for each IRC task.
- Measures of performance and effectiveness for each IRC task.
- Information required to assess each IRC task.

4-92. The COA worksheet needs to show how each IRC contributes to the IO objective and the scheme of IO for that COA. When completed, the work sheets help the IO officer tie together the staff products developed to support each COA. IO planners also use the worksheets to focus task development for all IRCs. They retain completed work sheets for use during subsequent steps of the MDMP.

Synchronization Matrix

4-93. The IO officer develops an IO synchronization matrix for each COA to determine when to execute IRC tasks. IO synchronization matrices show estimates of the time it takes for friendly forces to execute an IRC task; the adversary to observe, process and analyze the effect(s) of the executed task; and the adversary to act on those effect(s). The IO officer synchronizes IRC tasks with other combined arms tasks. The G-2 (S-2) and G-3 (S-3) time lines are used to reverse-plan and determine when to initiate IRC tasks. Due to the lead time required, some IRC tasks must be executed early in an operation. Regardless of when the IRC tasks start, they are still synchronized with other combined arms tasks. Many IRC tasks are executed throughout an operation; some are both first to begin and last to end. IO synchronization matrices vary in format, depending on commander preference and unit standard operating procedures. At a minimum, the synchronization matrix should include—

- IO objectives.
- IRC tasks.
- The operational timeline to execute the IRC tasks.
- The depiction of how IRC synchronization integrates with lines of operations or lines of effort.

Target Nominations

4-94. The IO officer uses information derived during mission analysis, IPB products, and the high-value target list to nominate high-pay-off targets (HPTs) for each friendly COA. HPTs are selected to be added to the high-payoff target list. HPTs are developed in conjunction with the IRC tasks employed to affect them. Targets attacked by nonlethal means, such as jamming or MISO broadcasts, may require assessment by means other than those normally used in battle damage assessment. The IO officer submits IRs for this information to the G-2 (S-2) when nominating them. If these targets are approved, the IRs needed to assess the effects on them become PIRs that the G-2 (S-2) adds to the information collection plan. If the command does not have the assets or resources to answer the IO IRs, the target is not engaged unless the attack guidance specifies otherwise or the commander so directs. The targeting team performs this synchronization.

Risk Assessment

4-95. The assessment of IO-associated risk during COA development and COA analysis focuses primarily on hazards related to executing the scheme of IO and its associated IRC tasks. However, the IO officer assesses all hazards as they emerge. The IO officer also monitors identified hazards and evaluates the effectiveness of controls established to counter them.

4-96. The IO officer examines each COA and its scheme of IO to determine if they contain hazards not identified during mission analysis. The IO officer then develops controls to manage these hazards, determines residual risk, and prepares to test the controls during COA analysis. The IO officer coordinates controls with other staff sections as necessary. Controls that require IRC tasks to implement are added to the IO COA worksheet for the COA.

4-97. The IO officer considers two types of hazards associated with the scheme of IO: those associated with the scheme of IO itself and its supporting IRC tasks; and those from other aspects of the concept of operations that may affect execution of IO. The IO officer identifies as many of these hazards as possible so the commander can consider them in decisions.

4-98. Some hazards result from the need to focus IO efforts. These hazards require commanders to take prudent risks. Some examples include:

- As part of a military deception operation, the commander limits camouflage, concealment, and deception measures applied to elements they want the adversary to detect. The commander accepts the risk of the threat targeting these elements.
- The commander concentrates cybersecurity efforts on a few critical mission command nodes, accepting the risk that other nodes may be degraded.
- The commander elects to destroy an adversary communications node that is also a valuable intelligence source. The commander accepts the risk of operating without that intelligence.

4-99. Hazards also result from unintended actions by the threat and other forces/groups in response to friendly IO. In addition, unintended consequences of other tactical activities can affect IO. Examples include:

- An electronic attack may disrupt friendly as well as threat communications.
- In a stability operation, efforts to influence a mayor to support U.S. forces instead of simply not opposing them may boost the popularity of an anti-U.S. rival, risking loss of long-term local political support.

4-100. Thorough planning can reduce, but will never eliminate, unintended consequences. The IO officer identifies possible unintended consequences that cause effects within the information environment and focuses on those most likely to affect mission accomplishment.

4-101. The IO officer considers the effects of IO-related hazards on the local populace and infrastructure as well as on friendly forces. The IO officer assesses these hazards, develops controls, determines residual risks, and advises the commander on risk mitigation measures. These unintended consequences could be caused by an IRC or by other activity that causes effects in the IE.

4-102. The commander alone accepts or rejects risk. The IO officer advises the commander concerning risk associated with IO-related hazards and recommends controls to mitigate this risk. The commander decides what risk to accept. An example of using IO for accident risk mitigation is the synchronized use of civil military operations and MISO, in coordination with public affairs, to warn the local populace of the accident hazards associated with military operations. When risks are attributable to IRC tasks, the IO officer assigns risk mitigation measures to the responsible unit and places them in the IO appendix's coordinating instructions.

4-103. The IO officer produces a list of IO-related hazards and assessments of the associated risks. This list becomes the IO input to the G-3 (S-3) risk assessment matrix. (For detailed information on assessing risk levels, see ATP 5-19.)

Measures of Performance and Effectiveness

4-104. Measures of performance and measures of effectiveness drive information requirements necessary to measure the degree to which operations accomplish the unit's mission. As COA development continues, the IO officer considers how to assess IO effectiveness, by determining:

- IRC tasks that require assessment.
- Measures of performance for IRC tasks and measures of effectiveness for IO objectives, as well as baselines to measure the degree of change, and associated IO-related targets.
- The information needed to make the assessment.

- How to collect the information.
- Who or what will collect the information.
- How the commander will use the information to support decisions.

4-105. The responses to these considerations are recorded on the IO COA worksheets and added to the IO portion of the operations assessment plan. Information required to assess IO effects becomes IRs. The IO officer submits IRs for the COA that the commander approves to the G-2 (S-2). The IO officer establishes measures of performance and effectiveness based on how IRC tasks contribute to achieving one or more IO objectives. If a task's results are not measurable, the IO officer eliminates the task.

ASSIGN HEADQUARTERS

4-106. Headquarters are typically assigned based on their ability to integrate the warfighting functions. Their capacity to plan, prepare, execute, and assess IO varies, depending on such variables as organic capabilities, mission essential tasks, and training. When commanders determines that the decisive operation or a shaping operation is IO-dominant, they turn to the IO officer to assess potential mission command vulnerabilities and ways to mitigate them. Higher headquarters, in particular, conduct this assessment for subordinate headquarters being assigned IO-dominant missions and provides additional assets, as required.

DEVELOP COURSE OF ACTION STATEMENTS AND SKETCHES

4-107. The G-3 (S-3) prepares a COA statement and supporting sketch for each COA for the overall operation. Together, the statement and sketch cover who, what, when, where, how, and why for each subordinate unit. They also state any significant risks for the force as a whole. The IO officer provides IO input to each COA statement and sketch. At a minimum, each COA statement and sketch should include its associated scheme of IO. COA statements may also identify select IO objectives and IRC tasks when they address specific commander concerns or priorities.

CONDUCT COURSE OF ACTION BRIEFING

4-108. Given the increasing impact of the information environment on operations, commanders benefit from ensuring the IO officer is present during all MDMP briefings. For this specific briefing, the IO officer is able to provide essential rationale for the scheme of IO and respond to IO-related questions from the commander or G-3 (S-3).

SELECT OR MODIFY COURSE OF ACTION FOR CONTINUED ANALYSIS

4-109. Whether the commander selects a given COA or COAs, modifies COAs, or creates a new COA altogether, the IO officer prepares for COA analysis and war-gaming. If the commander rejects all COAs, the IO officer develops new schemes of support, mindful of the commander's revised planning guidance.

4-110. Table 4-2 provides a summary of the inputs, actions and outputs required of the IO officer/element. Only those sub-steps within COA development with significant IO activity are listed.

Table 4-2. Course of action development

MDMP Sub-Step	Inputs	IO Officer Actions	IO Officer Outputs
Assess Relative Combat Power	• IPB or combined information overlay • Task organization • IO running estimate • Vulnerability assessment	**For each COA —** • Analyze IRC effects on friendly and threat capabilities, vulnerabilities, and combat power	**For each COA —** • Description of the potential effects of relative combat power stated by IRC

MDMP Sub-Step	Inputs	IO Officer Actions	IO Officer Outputs
Generate Options	• Commander's intent and guidance • IPB or combined information overlay • Friendly, neutral, and enemy information related capabilities, resources, and vulnerabilities	• Determine different ways for IO to support each COA • Determine IRCs to employ. • Determine how to focus IRCs on the overall objective • Determine IO's role in the decisive and shaping operations for each COA • Determine possible tradeoffs among IRCs • Develop input to military deception COAs (deception stories)	• Scheme of IO for each COA • Input to military deception COAs
Array Forces	• Restated mission • Commander's intent and guidance • IPB or combined information overlay • Input to military deception plan or concept	• Allocate IRCs for each scheme • Identify requirements for additional IRCs • Examine effect of possible military deception COAs on force positioning • Identify military deception means	• Initial IRC location and task organization • Additional IRC requirements

Table 4-2. Course of action development (continued)

MDMP Sub-Step	Inputs	IO Officer Actions	IO Officer Outputs
Develop a Broad Concept	• COAs • IPB or combined information overlay • High value target list • IO mission statement • Initial scheme of IO for each COA	**For each COA —** • Develop scheme of IO • Develop objectives • Develop control measures • Identify and prioritize IRC tasks • Nominate selected HPTs • Determine initial IO task execution timeline • Refine input to risk assessment • Develop IO portion of assessment plan • Identify additional EEFIs • Identify and assess OPSEC indicators to determine vulnerabilities • Develop OPSEC measures to shield vulnerabilities • Determine residual risk associated with each vulnerability after OPSEC measures are applied • Determine feedback required for assessment of military deception COAs	**For each COA —** • Refined scheme, objectives, and control measures; IRC tasks; and tasks to subordinate units • IO COA worksheets • Synchronization matrices • Execution time line • IO-related high-payoff target nominations • Critical and defended asset lists • Input to risk management plan, including residual risk associated with each OPSEC vulnerability • Success criteria to support assessment • Additional EEFIs • OPSEC vulnerabilities • OPSEC measures to shield vulnerabilities
Assign Headquarters	• IPB/combined information overlay • IO running estimate • IO vulnerability assessment • IO tasks by IRC and subordinate unit	**For each COA —** • Assess mission command strengths and weaknesses to determine vulnerabilities of specific headquarters regarding ability to execute IO • Assess mission command strengths and weaknesses to determine vulnerabilities of subordinate commands • Reevaluate critical and defended asset lists	**For each COA —** • Recommendations for allocation of G-3 (S-3) IO personnel to headquarters in light of mission command vulnerability assessment • Recommendations of grouping of IRCs to subordinate commands in light of mission command vulnerability assessment • Updated critical and defended asset lists • Initial list of IRCs to tasks assigned

Table 4-2. Course of action development (continued)

MDMP Sub-Step	Inputs	IO Officer Actions	IO Officer Outputs
Develop COA Statements and Sketches	• COA statement • A scheme of IO and objectives for each COA	• Submit input for each COA statement and sketch to G-3 (S-3) • Prepare scheme statement and sketch for each COA	• Input for each COA statement and sketch • Scheme of IO and sketches for each COA, stating the most important objectives

COA course of action	IO information operations	IPB intelligence preparation of the battlefield
EEFI essential element of friendly information	IPB intelligence preparation of the battlefield	OPSEC operations security
HPT high-payoff target	IRC information-related capability	

COURSE OF ACTION ANALYSIS AND WAR-GAMING

4-111. COA analysis (war-gaming) enables commanders and staffs to identify difficulties or coordination problems as well as probable consequences of planned actions for each COA being considered. It helps them think through the tentative plan. War-gaming is a disciplined process that staffs use to envision the flow of battle. Its purpose is to stimulate ideas and provide insights that might not otherwise be discovered. Effective war-gaming allows the staff to test each COA, identify its strengths and weaknesses, and alter it if necessary. During war-gaming, new hazards may be identified, the risk associated with them assessed, and controls established. OPSEC measures and other risk control measures are also evaluated.

4-112. War-gaming helps the IO officer synchronize IRC operations and helps the staff integrate IO into the overall operation. During the war game, the IO officer addresses how each IRC contributes to the scheme of IO for that COA and its associated time lines, critical events, and decision points. The IO officer revises the schemes of IO as needed during war-gaming.

4-113. The IO officer uses the synchronization matrices and worksheets for each COA as scripts for the war game. The IRCs are synchronized with each other and with the concepts of operations for the different COAs. To the extent possible, the IO officer also includes planned counter-actions to anticipated threat reactions.

4-114. During preparation for war-gaming, the IO officer gives the G-2 (S-2) likely threat information-related actions and reactions to friendly IO, to include possible threat responses in the information environment to friendly operations. The IO officer also continues to provide input to the G-2 (S-2) for HPT development and selection.

4-115. Before beginning the war game, staff planners develop criteria to evaluate the effectiveness and efficiency of each COA during COA comparison. These criteria are listed in paragraph 3c of the IO running estimate and become the outline for the COA analysis in paragraph 4. The IO officer develops the criteria for evaluating the schemes of IO. Using IO-specific criteria allows the IO officer to explain the advantages and disadvantages of each COA. Evaluation criteria that may help discriminate among various COAs could include:

● Lead time required for implementation.
● The number of decision points that require support.
● The cost of achieving an IO objective versus the expected benefits.
● The risk to friendly assets posed by threat information activities.

4-116. During war-gaming the IO officer participates in the action-reaction-counteraction process. For example, the action may be patrols designed to enforce curfew; the threat reaction is messaging accusing U.S. forces of causing damage and casualties; the counteraction is assigning combat camera to document U.S. force patrols and interactions with the indigenous population and incorporating the documentation with another IRC in order to provide appropriate content to the target audience. The IO officer uses the synchronization matrices and COA worksheets to insert IRC tasks into the war game at the time planned. A complete COA worksheet allows the IO officer to state the organization performing the task and its location. The IO officer remains flexible throughout the process and is prepared to modify input to the war game as it develops. The IO officer is also prepared to modify the scheme of IO, IO objectives, and IRC tasks to mitigate possible threat actions discovered during the war game. The IO officer notes any branches and sequels identified during the war game. Concepts of support for these branches or sequels are developed as time permits.

4-117.   The results of COA analysis are a refined scheme of IO and associated products for each COA. During war-gaming, the IO officer refines IRs, EEFIs, and HPTs for each COA, synchronizing them with that COA's concept of operations. Staff planners normally record war-gaming results, including IRC effects, on the G-3 (S-3) synchronization matrix. The IO officer may also record the results on the COA worksheets. These help the IO officer subsequently synchronize IRCs. The worksheets and synchronization matrices provide the basis for IO input to paragraph 3 of the OPLAN/OPORD, paragraph 3 of the IO and IRC appendices.

4-118.   Table 4-3 on page 4-27 provides a summary of the inputs, actions and outputs required of the IO officer during course of action analysis.

COURSE OF ACTION COMPARISON

4-119.   During COA comparison, the staff compares feasible COAs to identify the one with the highest probability of success against the most likely adversary COA and the most dangerous adversary COA. Each staff section evaluates the advantages and disadvantages of each COA from the staff section's perspective, and presents its findings to the staff. The staff outlines each COA in terms of the evaluation criteria established before the war game and identifies the advantages and disadvantages of each with respect to the others. The IO officer records this analysis in paragraph 4 of the IO estimate.

4-120.   The IO officer determines the COA that IO can best support based on the evaluation criteria established during war-game preparation. The results of this comparison become paragraph 5 of the IO estimate.

4-121.   Table 4-4 on page 4-28 provides a summary of the inputs, actions and outputs required of the IO officer during course of action comparison. Table 4-3. Course of action analysis (war game)

Table 4-3. Course of action analysis (war game)

MDMP Step	Inputs	IO Officer Actions	IO Officer Outputs
Course of Action Analysis	• Updated running estimate. • IPB/combined information overlay • Updated assumptions **For each COA —** • Scheme of IO and objectives for each COA sketch • Execution timeline	• Develop evaluation criteria for each COA • Gather the tools • List all friendly IRCs • List assumptions • Synchronize tasks performed by different IRCs and subordinate commands • Coordinate IO with cyber electromagnetic activities • Integrate scheme of IO into the concept of operations for each COA • Synchronize scheme of IO with higher and adjacent headquarters • Identify enemy information warfare capabilities and likely actions and reactions • War game friendly IRCs against enemy vulnerabilities and display the results • War game friendly IRC impacts on various audiences and populations and display the results • War game enemy information warfare capabilities against friendly vulnerabilities and display the results • Synchronize and de-conflict targets • Determine whether modifications to the COA result in additional EEFIs or OPSEC vulnerabilities; if so recommend OPSEC measures to shield them • Assign attack measures to HPTs. • Test OPSEC measures • Determine decision points for executing tasks • War game each military deception COA • Identify each military deception COA's potential branches; assess risk to the COA • List the most dangerous or beneficial branch on the decision support template or synchronization matrix • Participate in the war game briefing (optional)	• Potential decision points • Initial assessment measures • Updated assumptions • An evaluation of each military deception COA in terms of criteria established before the war game **For each COA —** • An evaluation in terms of criteria established before the war game • Recorded input to war game results • Refined scheme of IO • Refined tasks • Refined input to attack guidance matrix and target support matrix • IRs and requests for information identified during war game • Refined EEFIs and OPSEC vulnerabilities and OPSEC measures • Paragraph 4 of the running estimate • Input to the G-3 (S-3) synchronization matrix • Input to the HPTL

COA course of action	**IPB** intelligence preparation of the battlefield
EEFIs essential elements of friendly information	**IR** information requirement
HPT high-payoff target	**IRC** information-related capability
HPTL high-payoff target list	**OPSEC** operations security
IO information operations	**MDMP** military decisionmaking process

Table 4-4. COA comparison

MDMP Task	Inputs	IO Officer Actions	IO Officer Outputs
Course of Action Comparison	• Updated IO running estimate • Refined COAs • COA evaluation criteria • COA evaluations from COA analysis • Updated assumptions	• Compare the COAs with each other to determine the advantages and disadvantages of each • Determine which COA is most supportable from an IO perspective • Determine if any OPSEC measures require the commander's approval	• Advantages and disadvantages for each COA • Most supportable COA from an IO perspective • Input to COA decision matrix • Updated assumptions • Paragraph 4, IO running estimate
COA course of action	**IO** information operations	**MDMP** military decisionmaking process	**OPSEC** operations security

COURSE OF ACTION APPROVAL

4-122.   After completing the COA comparison, the staff identifies its preferred COA and recommends it to the commander in a COA decision briefing, if time permits. The concept of operations for the approved COA becomes the concept of operations for the operation itself. The scheme of IO for the approved COA becomes the scheme of IO for the operation. Once a COA is approved, the commander refines the commander's intent and issues additional planning guidance. The G-3 (S-3) then issues a WARNORD and begins orders production.

4-123.   The WARNORD issued after COA approval contains information that executing units require to complete planning and preparation. Possible IO input to this WARNORD includes:
- Contributions to the commander's intent/concept of operations.
- Changes to the CCIRs.
- Additional or modified risk guidance.
- Time-sensitive reconnaissance tasks.
- IRC tasks requiring early initiation.
- A summary of the scheme of IO and IO objectives.

4-124.   During the COA decision briefing, the IO officer is prepared to present the associated scheme of IO for each COA and comment on the COA from an IO perspective. If the IO officer perceives the need for additions or changes to the commander's intent or guidance with respect to IO, they ask for it.

4-125.   Table 4-5 on page 4-29 provides a summary of the inputs, actions and outputs required of the IO officer during course of action approval.

ORDERS PRODUCTION, DISSEMINATION, AND TRANSITION

4-126.   Based on the commander's decision and final guidance, the staff refines the approved COA and completes and issues the OPLAN/OPORD. Time permitting, the staff begins planning branches and sequels. The IO officer ensures input is placed in the appropriate paragraphs of the base order and its annexes, especially the IO appendix to the operations annex. When necessary, the IO officer or appropriate special staff officers prepare appendixes for one or more IRCs [(See Appendix A for an annotated format of appendix 15 (Information Operations) to Annex C (Operations)].

4-127. Table 4-6 provides a summary of the inputs, actions and outputs required of the IO officer during course of action approval.

Table 4-5. Course of action approval

MDMP Step	Inputs	IO Officer Actions	IO Officer Outputs
Course of Action Approval	• Updated IO running estimate • Evaluated COAs • Recommended COAs • Updated assumptions	• Provide input to COA recommendation • Re-evaluate input to the commander's intent and guidance • Refine scheme of IO, objectives, and tasks for approved COA and update synchronization matrix • Prepare input to the WARNORD • Participate in the COA decision briefing • Recommend the COA that IO can best support • Request decision on executing any OPSEC measures that entail significant resource expenditure or high risk	• Finalized scheme of IO for approved COA • Finalized tasks based on approved COA • Input to WARNORD • Updated synchronization matrix

COA course of action IO information operations MDMP military decisionmaking process WARNORD warning order

Table 4-6. Orders production, dissemination and transition

MDMP Task	Inputs	IO Officer Actions	IO Officer Outputs
Orders Production, Dissemination and Transition	• Approved COA • Refined commander's guidance • Refined commander's intent • IO running estimate • Execution matrix • Finalized mission statement, scheme of IO, objectives, and tasks	• Ensure input is placed in tasks to subordinate units and coordinating instructions • Produce Appendix 14 (MILDEC) to Annex C (Operations) • Produce Appendix 15 (IO) to Annex C (Operations) • Produce Appendix 3 (OPSEC) to Annex E (Protection) • Coordinate tasks with IRC staff officers • Conduct other staff coordination. • Refine execution matrix • Transition from planning to operations	• Synchronization matrix • Approved Paragraph 3.k. (10) • Approved Appendix 14 to Annex C • Approved Appendix 15 to Annex C • Approved Appendix 3 to Annex E • IO input to AGM and TSM • Subordinates understand the IO portion of the plan or order

AGM attack guidance matrix COA course of action IO information operations IRC information-related capability MDMP military decisionmaking process MILDEC military deception OPSEC operations security TSM trunk signaling mission

Other books we publish on Amazon.com

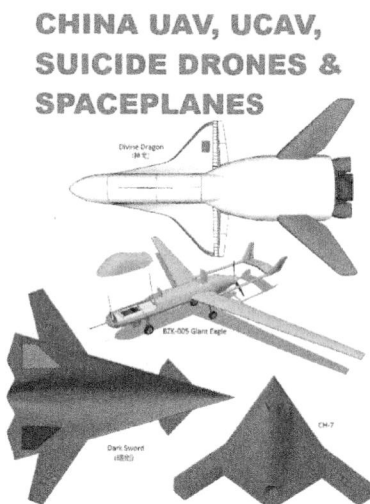

Chapter 5

Preparation

5-1. Preparation consists of those activities performed by units and Soldiers to improve their ability to execute an operation (ADP 5-0). Preparation creates conditions that improve friendly force opportunities for success. Because many IO objectives and IRC tasks require long lead times to create desired effects, preparation for IO often starts earlier than for other types of operations. Initial preparation for specific IRCs and IO units (such as 1st IO Command or a Theater IO Group) may begin during peacetime.

5-2. Peacetime preparation by units or capabilities involves building contingency plan databases about the anticipated area of operations. These databases can be used for IO input to IPB and to plan IO to defend friendly intentions, such as network protection and operations security (OPSEC). IO portions of contingency plans are continuously updated. Normal IO working group participants maintain their own data to provide the IO officer with the latest information.

5-3. During peacetime, IO officers prepare for future operations by analyzing anticipated area(s) of operations' information environment and likely threat information capabilities. Examples of factors to consider include, but are not limited to—

- Religious, ethnic, and cultural mores, norms, and values.
- Non-military communications infrastructure and architecture.
- Military communication and command and control infrastructure and architecture.
- Military training and level of proficiency (to determine susceptibility to denial, deception, and IO).
- Literacy rate.
- Formal and informal organizations exerting influence and leaders within these organizations.
- Ethnic factional relationships and languages.

5-4. Preparation includes assessing unit readiness to execute IO. Commanders and staffs monitor preparations and evaluate them against criteria established during planning to determine variances. This assessment forecasts the effects these factors have on readiness to execute the overall operation as well as individual IRC tasks.

5-5. Preparation for IO takes place at three levels: staff (IO officer), IRC units or elements, and individual. The IO officer helps prepare for IO by performing staff tasks and monitoring preparations by IRC units or elements. These units perform preparation activities as a group for tasks that involve the entire unit, and as individuals for tasks that each soldier and leader must complete.

5-6. Chapter 3 of ADRP 5-0 provides a comprehensive overview of preparation activities. The activities most relevant to conducting IO include—

- Improve situational understanding.
- Revise and refine plans and orders.
- Conduct coordination and liaison.
- Initiate information collection.
- Initiate security operations.
- Initiate troop movements.
- Initiate network preparation.
- Manage and prepare terrain.
- Conduct confirmation briefs.
- Conduct rehearsals.

IMPROVE SITUATIONAL UNDERSTANDING

5-7. The IO officer/element must understand and share their understanding of the information environment with the commander and staff. During preparation, information collection begins, which helps to validate assumptions and improve situational understanding. Coordination, liaison, and rehearsals further enhance this understanding. Given the information environment's complexity, this task is never-ending and depends on everyone, not just the IO officer, to update and refine understanding of the information environment.

REVISE AND REFINE PLANS AND ORDERS

5-8. Plans are not static; the commander adjusts them based on new information. This information may be the result of analysis of unit preparations, answers to IO IRs, and updates of threat information capacity and capability.

5-9. During preparation, the IO officer adjusts the relevant portions of the operation plan (OPLAN) or operation order (OPORD) to reflect the commander's decisions. The IO officer also updates the IO running estimate so that it contains the most current information about adversary information activities, changes in the weather or terrain, and friendly IRCs.

5-10. The IO officer ensures that IO input to IPB remains relevant throughout planning and preparation. To do this, they ensure that IO input to the information collection plan is adjusted to support refinements and revisions made to the OPLAN/OPORD.

5-11. IO preparation begins during planning. As the IO appendix begins to take shape, IO officer coordination with other staff elements is vital because IO affects every other warfighting function. For example, planning an attack on a command and control (C2) high-payoff target requires coordination with the targeting team. A comprehensive attack offering a high probability of success may involve air interdiction and therefore needs to be placed on the air tasking order. It may involve deep attack: rocket and missile fires have to be scheduled in the fire support plan. Army jammers and collectors have to fly the missions when and where needed. The IO officer ensures the different portions of the OPLAN/OPORD contain the necessary coordinating instructions for these actions to occur at the right time and place.

5-12. Effective IO is consistent at all echelons. The IO officer reviews subordinate unit OPLANs/OPORDs to ensure IO has been effectively addressed and detect inconsistencies. The IO officer also looks for possible conflicts between the command's OPLAN/OPORD and those of subordinates. When appropriate, the IO officer reviews adjacent unit OPLANs/OPORDs for possible conflicts. This review allows the IO officer to identify opportunities to mass IO effects across units.

5-13. OPLAN/OPORD refinement includes developing branches and sequels. Branches and sequels are normally identified during war-gaming (COA analysis). However, the staff may determine the need for them at any time. The G-3 (S-3) prioritizes branches and sequels. The staff develops them as time permits. The IO officer participates in their development as with any other aspect of planning.

5-14. A key focus during preparation is on assessment of the current state of the information environment. This assessment is performed to establish baselines, which are subsequently used when assessing whether IO objectives and IRC tasks were effective in creating desired effects.

CONDUCT COORDINATION AND LIAISON

5-15. IO requires all units and elements to coordinate with each other continuously, as well as liaise. Coordination begins during planning; however, input to a plan alone does not constitute coordination. Coordination involves exchanging the information needed to synchronize operations. The majority of coordination takes place during preparation. It is then that the IO officer follows through on the coordination initiated during planning. Exchanging information is critical to successful coordination and execution. Coordination may be internal or external and is enhanced through liaison.

INTERNAL COORDINATION

5-16. Internal coordination occurs within the unit headquarters. The IO officer initiates the explicit and implicit coordinating activities with other staff sections, as well as within the IO element, if one exists. Much of this coordination occurs during IO working group meetings; however, IO working group members do not wait for a meeting to coordinate. They remain aware of actions that may affect, or be affected by, their functional responsibilities. They initiate coordination as soon as they become aware of a situation that requires it. The IO officer remains fully informed of IO-related coordination. The IO officer corrects or resolves problems of external coordination revealed by command and staff visits and information gathering. During internal coordination, the IO officer resolves problems and conflicts and ensures that resources allocated to support IO arrive and are distributed. Examples of internal coordination include, but are not limited to:

- Deconflicting military information support operations (MISO) with public affairs activities and products.
- Monitoring the progress of answers to IO RFIs.
- Monitoring RFIs to higher headquarters by the G-3 (S-3) current operations.
- Checking the air tasking order for missions requested by the IO officer/element.
- Monitoring the movements and readiness of IRCs.
- Determining space asset status and space weather implications.
- Participating in the integration of IO-related targets into the targeting process.
- Continuous monitoring and validation of OPSEC procedures, particularly in preparation for military deception. This could include a short statement on physical security, particularly during movement.

5-17. The IO officer remains mindful that training is conducted during planning and preparation. This training occurs as new soldiers and IRCs are integrated into the command and its battle rhythm. Additionally, the IO officer provides training to subordinate elements, as requested, to fill gaps in their IO capacity.

5-18. Internal coordination is especially important to ensure requisite staff support to various IRCs in order to enhance their readiness and effectiveness. Examples include but are not limited to—

- Electronic warfare (EW).
    - G-2 (S-2)—Coordinates intelligence gathering in support of the EW mission. Recommend the use of EW against adversary systems that use the electromagnetic spectrum.
    - G-3 (S-3)—Coordinates and prioritizes EW targets.
    - G-4 (S-4)—Coordinates distribution of EW equipment and supplies, less cryptographic support.
    - IO officer—Coordinates EW tasks with those of other IRCs and assists with preparation of the cyberspace electromagnetic activities appendix.
    - EW officer—Monitors the preparation of military intelligence units to support EW missions; prepare cyber effects request forms and electronic attack request forms; monitors other staff functions that support or affect EW.
- MISO.
    - G-2 (S-2)—Prepares intelligence estimate and analysis of the area of operation.
    - G-3 (S-3)—Requests additional MISO units as required.
    - IO officer—Identifies requirements for additional MISO units to the G-3 (S-3).
    - G-4 (S-4)—Prepares logistic support of MISO.
    - Psychological Operations (PSYOP) officer—Prepares the MISO appendix to Annex C. Prepares the MISO estimate.
- OPSEC.
    - G-2(S-2)—Provides data on threat intelligence collection capabilities.
    - IO officer—Determines the EEFIs.
    - G-4 (S-4)—Advises on the vulnerabilities of supply, transport, and maintenance facilities, and lines of communications.

- G-5 (S-5)—Determines availability of civilian resources for use as guard forces.
- OPSEC officer—Prepares the OPSEC estimate and appendix.
- Provost marshal—Advises on physical security measures.
- Military deception.
  - G-2 (S-2)—Determines adversary surveillance capabilities.
  - G-3 (S-3)—Coordinates movement of units participating in military deception.
  - G-4 (S-4)—Coordinates logistic support to carry out assigned deception tasks.
  - G-9 (S-9)—Coordinates host-nation support to implement the military deception plan.
  - Military deception officer—Prepares to monitor execution of military deception operation.

EXTERNAL COORDINATION

5-19. External coordination includes coordinating with or among subordinate units and higher headquarters, as well as IO support units, IRCs, and resources that may not be under the unit's control during planning but are necessary to execute the plan. External coordination also includes coordinating with adjacent units or agencies. (Adjacent refers to any organization that can affect a unit's operations in and through the information environment.) This coordination is necessary to integrate IO throughout the force. Examples of external coordination include:

- Assessing unit OPSEC posture.
- Making sure the military deception operation is tracking with preparation for the overall operation.
- Periodically validating assumptions.
- Ensuring military deception operations are synchronized with those of higher, lower, and adjacent units.

5-20. The IO officer remains aware of the effectiveness of cybersecurity tasks taken by the G-6 (S-6). Proper protection of plans and orders, and refinements to them, are essential during operations.

5-21. Coordination with joint, interorganizational, and multinational partners is essential to the conduct of IO, as these entities and organizations affect the information environment and are affected by it. The IO working group is the primary means for this coordination but direct, face-to-face coordination is frequently necessary to ensure unity of effort.

LIAISON

5-22. Establishing and maintaining liaison is one of the most important means of external coordination. The IO officer may perform direct liaison but units may select another staff member to be part of the liaison team. Establishing liaison during planning enhances subsequent coordination during preparation and execution.

5-23. Practical liaison can be achieved through personal contact between IO officers or between the IO officer and agencies/organizations involved in affecting the information environment. This coordination is accomplished through exchanging personnel, through agreement on mutual support between adjacent units or organizations, or by a combination of these means. Liaison should, when possible, be reciprocal between higher, lower, and adjacent units/organizations. Liaison must be reciprocal between IO sections when U.S. forces are operating with or adjacent to multinational partners.

5-24. Liaison also has a force protection mission. Where host-nation security forces retain some operational capability, liaison is vital to coordinate actions. They provide intelligence and other related information about conditions in-theater.

INITIATE INFORMATION COLLECTION

5-25. Execution requires accurate, up-to-date situational awareness. During preparation, the IO officer updates IRs to ensure the most current information possible. The IO officer also works with the G-2 (S-2) to update collection asset taskings necessary to assess IO.

INITIATE SECURITY OPERATIONS

5-26. Security operations serve to protect the force from surprise and threat attacks during preparation. While often considered in terms of specific missions that physically screen, guard, cover, or provide area or local security, security operations should also include IRC tasks that provide these same protections in the informational and cognitive dimensions of the information environment. Military deception, OSPEC, space operations, and cyberspace operations all support security operations. Not including these IRC effects into plans potentially puts the force at risk.

INITIATE TROOP MOVEMENTS

5-27. During preparation, IRCs are positioned or repositioned, as necessary, to ensure they can fulfill their assigned tasks. IO unit augmentation and integration also occurs during preparation.

INITIATE NETWORK PREPARATION

5-28. IO supports the commander's ability to optimize the information element of combat power. In terms of establishing and readying the network, units must think in terms of both technical and human networks. Technical networks have to be set up, engineered, tailored, and tested to meet the specific needs of each operation. Similarly, human networks have to be initiated, cultivated, and refined during preparation. The IO officer coordinates the establishment of networks that help shape the information environment favorable to friendly objectives. The goal of establishing each category of network is to ensure the availability, reliability, accuracy, and speed of information to facilitate shared understanding and decision making.

MANAGE AND PREPARE TERRAIN

5-29. *Terrain management* is the process of allocating terrain by establishing areas of operation, designating assembly areas, and specifying locations for units and activities to deconflict activities that might interfere with each other (ADRP 5-0). While terrain is physical and geographic, it is a subset of the operational and information environments. When commanders designate areas of operation, they are simultaneously assigning responsibility to specific portions of the information environment. One of the most important reasons for managing physical terrain is to avoid fratricide. The same rationale exists for the information environment: to avoid information fratricide. For example, the IO officer can ensure control measures are established to deconflict EW activities with MISO efforts to inform the local populace through radio broadcasts.

5-30. Analysis of the information environment during IPB leads to an understanding of aspects of the information environment in which friendly forces have an advantage and in which they are disadvantaged. During preparation, the IO officer, in concert with the IO working group and its members, undertake actions to exploit the advantages and overcome the disadvantages. For example, if cellular phone communication is essential to strengthen coordination between U.S. forces and an indigenous ally and cell towers are non-existent or degraded, mobile towers could be deployed.

CONDUCT CONFIRMATION BRIEFINGS

5-31. A confirmation brief is a briefing subordinate leaders give to the higher commander immediately after the operation order is given. It is the leaders' understanding of the commander's intent, their specific tasks, and the relationship between their mission and the other units in the operation. The IO officer assists subordinate commanders and their IO representatives with these briefings when the commander's intent and specific tasks are IO-focused or have aspects related to IO. They also assist subordinate commanders to deduce IO implied tasks and to understand the information environment in their area of operations.

CONDUCT REHEARSALS

5-32. The IO officer participates in unit rehearsals to ensure IO is integrated with overall operation and to identify potential problems during execution. The IO officer may conduct further rehearsals of tasks and actions to ensure coordination and effective synchronization of IRCs. Before participating in a rehearsal, the IO officer reviews the plans or orders of subordinate and supporting commands.

Chapter 6

Execution

6-1. Execution of IO includes IRCs executing the synchronization plan and the commander and staff monitoring and assessing their activities relative to the plan and adjusting these efforts, as necessary. The primary mechanism for monitoring and assessing IRC activities is the IO working group. There are two variations of the IO working group. The first monitors and assesses ongoing planned operations and convenes on a routine, recurring basis. The second monitors and assesses unplanned or crisis situations and convenes on an as-needed basis.

INFORMATION OPERATIONS WORKING GROUP

6-2. The IO working group is the primary means by which the commander, staff and other relevant participants ensure the execution of IO. The IO working group is a collaborative staff meeting led by the IO officer, and periodically chaired by the G-3 (S-3), executive officer, chief of staff or the commander. It is a critical planning event integrated into the unit's battle rhythm. Figure 6-1 on page 6-2 provides a possible template for the conduct of the IO working group that can be applied at the tactical through strategic levels. Core and other participants are not static; they will fluctuate by level and by mission/situation.

PURPOSE

6-3. The IO working group is the primary mechanism for ensuring effects in and through the information environment are planned and synchronized to support the commander's intent and concept of operations. This means that the staff must assess the current status of operations relative to the end state and determine where efforts are working well and where they are not. More specifically, they must ensure targets are identified and nominated at the right place and time to achieve decisive results. The IO working group occurs regularly in the unit's battle rhythm and always before the next targeting working group. The only exception is a crisis IO working group (also referred to as consequence management or crisis action working group), which occurs as soon as feasible before or after an event or incident that will significantly alter the information environment and give the threat operational advantage unless handled quickly and adeptly.

INPUTS/OUTPUTS

6-4. The example in figure 6-1 is not exhaustive. In terms of inputs, it identifies those documents, products, and tools that historically and practically have provided the IO working group the information necessary to achieve consensus and make informed recommendations to the G-3 (S-3) and commander. The outputs listed are those considered essential to ensuring the staff can effectively conduct IO.

6-5. One tool that the IO working group uses to affirm and adjust the synchronized employment of IRCs is the IO synchronization matrix. An updated synchronization matrix is the working group's key output and essential input to the next targeting meeting.

AGENDA

6-6. Like other aspects of the IO working group, the proposed agenda is flexible to the needs of the commander and the staff/participants. Figure 6-1 breaks the meeting down by weighted effort, recognizing that some members of the working group may not need to participate in all parts and that classification levels may adjust depending on the capabilities or assets under consideration and discussion. For example, the public affairs officer/representative will likely be present for Parts 1, 2 and possibly 3, but not for Part 4. Another possible agenda format is by time horizon and yet another by phase of the operation.

Purpose	Agenda
Prioritize, request, and synchronize information-related capabilities and IO augmentation to optimize effects in and through the IE. **Battle Rhythm:** • Before targeting work group	Part 1: Operations and Intelligence Update • Intelligence update • Information environment update • Operations update or significant activities • Review plans, future operations, and current operations • Assessment update (information requirements, indicators) • Calendar update, due outs, and responsibilities from previous meeting **Part 2:** Stabilize • Review and update **Part 3:** Protect and defend synch matrix **Part 4:** Attack • Guidance and comments

Inputs/Outputs		Structure/Participants
Inputs: • Higher headquarters orders and guidance • Commander's intent, concept of operations and narrative • Information-related capabilities status (running estimates) • Intelligence collection assets • Combined information overlays, intelligence preparation of the battlefield • Media monitoring analysis • Cultural calendar • Engagements schedule • Audience analysis • Scheme of IO and synchronization matrix • Commander's objectives for IO • Success criteria: measures of effectiveness and performance	**Outputs:** • Updated scheme of IO • Updated IO synchronization matrix • Key leader engagement recommendations • Refined themes and messages • Refined operational products • Target nominations • Updated combined information overlay • Plans and orders update • Information requirements	**Lead:** IO Officer (chair: G-3 (S-3), XO, DCO, or CDR) **Core participants:** Military information support operations, G-2 (S-2), subordinate unit representatives, G-3 (S-3), fires, G-9 (S-9), operations security, public affairs **Other participants:** G-6 (S-6), cyber electromagnetic activities, space operations, military deception planner, combat camera, foreign area officer or cultural advisor, special forces liaison, knowledge management officer, G-4 (S-4), engineer, chaplain, staff judge advocate, chaplain and unified action partners (mission and situation dependent)

CCIR commander's critical information requirements **CDR** commander **DCO** defense coordinating officer **EEFI** essential elements of friendly information **G-2** assistant chief of staff, intelligence **G-3** assistant chief of staff, operations	**G-4** assistant chief of staff, logistics **G-6** assistant chief of staff, signal **G-9** assistant chief of staff, civil affairs operations **IE** information environment **IO** information operations	**IPB** intelligence preparation of the battlefield **IRCs** information-related capabilities **OPSEC** operations security **S-2** battalion or brigade intelligence staff officer **S-3** battalion or brigade operations staff officer	**S-4** battalion or brigade logistics staff officer **S-6** battalion or brigade signal staff officer **S-9** battalion or brigade civil affairs operations staff officer

Figure 6-1: Example template for an IO working group

6-7.   Consistent across all agenda formats are the operational and intelligence updates. These updates are designed to ground participants in the current situation and threat, examine how well operations are meeting the concept of operations and determine whether results are advancing the unit toward the desired end state.

STRUCTURE/PARTICIPANTS

6-8.   The IO officer leads and routinely chairs the IO working group. Staff members typically participating in the working group include personnel from the warfighting functional cells (as appropriate to the mission), the coordinating cells, the special staff, IRC managers (organic and augmenting), subordinate unit IO officers, and augmenting IO units or teams. Table 6-1 on page 6-4 provides an example listing of the participants as well as sample responsibilities.

IO WORKING GROUP IN ANTICIPATION OF/RESPONSE TO CRISIS OR SIGNIFICANT INCIDENT

6-9.   The IO working group convenes as soon as feasible before or after an event. Anyone can request the convening of the IO working group to deal with crisis or incident through the IO officer who, in consultation with the G-3 (S-3) and commander, determines the merits of the request and those personnel who should comprise the working group's initial membership. The working group's purpose is to determine the additional measures, activities, and effects that must be undertaken or generated in order to sustain operational advantage in the information environment. The group also seeks to mitigate possible negative consequences resulting from crisis events or incidents, particularly those that would adversely affect U.S. and coalition credibility. Its membership is more ad-hoc than the routine IO working group but also situation dependent.

IO RESPONSIBILITIES WITHIN THE VARIOUS COMMAND POSTS

6-10. IO execution involves monitoring and assessing IO as the operation unfolds and requires coordination among the tactical command post (CP) and main CP, which can be challenging. Each monitors different parts of the operation and not all have an assigned functional area 30 or IO officer. Continuous exchange of information among those assigned responsibility for IO at these CPs is essential to ensuring the effective execution of IO.

6-11. The tactical CP directs IO execution and adjusts missions as required. The IO representative or responsible agent—

- Maintains the IO portion of the common operational picture to support current operations.
- Maintains information requirement status.
- Coordinates preparation and execution of IO with maneuver and fires.
- Recommends adjustments to current IO.
- Tracks IRCs and recommends repositioning, as required.
- Tracks applicable targets in conjunction with the G-2 (S-2).
- Nominates targets for attack.
- Provides initial assessment of effectiveness.

6-12. The main CP plans, coordinates, and integrates IO. It—

- Creates and maintains IO aspects of the common operational picture.
- Maintains the IO estimate.
- Incorporates answers to IRs and requests for information into the IO estimate.
- Maintains a current IO order of battle.
- Deconflicts IO internally and externally.
- Requests/coordinates IO support with other warfighting function representatives, outside agencies, higher headquarters, and augmenting forces.
- Identifies future objectives based on successes or failures of current operations.

Table 6-1. Roles and responsibilities of IO working group representatives

Representative	Responsibility
Information Operations	<ul><li>Distribute read-ahead packets</li><li>Lead working group</li><li>Establish and enforce agenda</li><li>Lead information environment update</li><li>Recommend commander's critical information requirements</li><li>Keep records, track tasks, and disseminate meeting notes</li></ul>
Cyber Electromagnetic Activities	<ul><li>Provide cyber electromagnetic activities-related information and capabilities to support information operations analysis and objectives</li><li>Coordinate, synchronize and deconflict information operations efforts with cyberspace electromagnetic activities efforts or cyberspace electromagnetic activities efforts with information operations efforts</li></ul>

Table 6.1. Roles and responsibilities of IO working group representatives (continued)

Representative	Responsibility
Military Information Support Operations	• Advise on both psychological effects (planned) and psychological impacts (unplanned) • Advise on use of lethal and nonlethal means to influence selected audiences to accomplish objectives • Develop key leader engagement plans • Monitor and coordinate assigned, attached, or supporting military information support unit actions • Identify status of influence efforts in the unit, laterally, and at higher and lower echelons • Provide target audience analysis
G-2 (S-2)	• Provide an intelligence update • Brief information requirements and priority information requirements • Develop the initial information collection plan • Provide foreign disclosure-related guidance and updates
G-3 (S-3)	• Provide operations update and significant activity update • Task units or sections based on due outs • Update fragmentary orders • Maintain a task tracker
Subordinate unit information operations	• Identify opportunities for information operations support to lines of effort • Provide input to assessments • Provide input to information environment update
Public Affairs	• Develop media analysis products • Develop media engagement plan • Provide higher headquarters strategic communication plan • Provide changes to themes and messages from higher headquarters • Develop command information plan
G-9 (S-9)	• Provides specific country information • Ensures the timely update of the civil component of the common operational picture through the civil information management process • Advise on civil considerations within the operational environment • Identify concerns of population groups within the projected joint operational area/area of operations and potential flash points that can result in civil instability • Provide cultural awareness briefings • Advise on displaced civilians movement routes, critical infrastructure, and significant social, religious, and cultural shrines, monuments, and facilities • Advise on information impacts on the civil component • Identify key civilian nodes
Information-related capabilities representatives	• Serve as subject-matter expert for their staff function or capability • Identify opportunities for information-related capability support to lines of effort or operations

G-2 assistant chief of staff, intelligence	**G-9** assistant chief of staff, civil affairs operations	**S-3** battalion or brigade operations staff officer
G-3 assistant chief of staff, operations	**S-2** battalion or brigade intelligence staff officer	**S-9** battalion or brigade civil affairs operations staff officer

6-13. The IO officer monitors IRCs and keeps the G-3 (S-3) informed on overall IO status. The IO officer also recommends to the G-3 (S-3) changes to IRC taskings for inclusion in fragmentary orders, as warranted.

ASSESSING DURING EXECUTION

6-14. Assessment precedes and guides the other activities of the operations process. It involves continuous monitoring of the current situation and evaluation of the current situation against the desired end state to determine progress and make decisions and adjustments.

6-15. The IO officer compiles information from all CPs, the G-2 (S-2), and higher headquarters to maintain a continuous IO assessment in the IO estimate. The primary objective of assessment is to determine whether IO is achieving planned effects. As the situation changes, the IO officer and G-3 (S-3) make sure IO remains fully synchronized with the overall operation.

6-16. Assessment is continuous; it precedes and guides every operations process activity and concludes each operation or phase of an operation. During planning, the commander and staff determine those IO objectives to be assessed, measures of performance and effectiveness, and the means of obtaining the information necessary to determine effectiveness. During orders production, the IO officer uses this information to prepare the IO portion of the overall assessment plan. During execution, the IO officer uses established measures of performance and effectiveness, as well as baselines and indicators, to assess IO objectives.

MONITORING IO

6-17. The IO officer monitors IRCs to determine progress towards achieving the IO objectives. Once execution begins, the IO officer monitors the threat and friendly situations to track IRC task accomplishment, determine the effects of IO during each phase of the operation, and detect and track any unintended consequences.

6-18. Monitoring the execution of defend-weighted tasks is done at the main CP because it is the focal point for intelligence analysis and production, and because the headquarters mission command nodes are monitored there. The IO officer works closely with the intelligence cell, G-2 (S-2), and IO working group representatives to provide a running assessment of the effectiveness of threat information efforts and keeps the G-3 (S-3) and various integrating cells informed.

6-19. With G-2 (S-2), G-3 (S-3), and fire support representatives, the IO officer monitors attack-weighted IO execution in the tactical CP and the main CP. For example, during combined arms maneuver, the IO officer is concerned with attacking threat command and control nodes with airborne and ground-based jammers, fire support, attack helicopters, and tactical air. After preplanned IO-related HPTs have been struck, the strike's effectiveness is assessed. Effective IO support of current operations depends on how rapidly the tactical CP can perform the targeting cycle to strike targets of opportunity. The G-3 (S-3) representative in the tactical CP keeps the main CP informed of current operations, including IO.

6-20. To organize and portray IO execution, the IO officer and working group use several tools, to include:
- IO synchronization matrix.
- Decision support template.
- High-payoff target list.
- Critical asset list and defended asset list.

6-21. IO officer and working group use either the synchronization matrix from the IO appendix or an extract containing current and near-term IO objectives and IRC tasks, depending on the complexity of the operation. The synchronization matrix is used to monitor progress and results of IO objectives and IRC tasks and keep IO execution focused on contributing to the overall operation. The decision support template produced by the G-3 (S-3) is used by the IO officer to monitor progress of IO in relation to decision points and any branches or sequels. The IO officer maintains a list or graphic (for example, a link and node diagram) that tracks the status of IO-related HPTs identified during planning. The IO officer uses the critical asset list and defended asset list to monitor the status of critical friendly information nodes and the status of critical systems supporting IO, for example: electronic warfare systems, military information support operations (MISO) assets, and deep attack assets.

EVALUATING IO

6-22. During execution, the IO officer works with the intelligence cell and integrating cells to obtain the information needed to determine individual and collective IO effects. Evaluation not only estimates the effectiveness of task execution, but also evaluates the effect of the entire IO effort on the threat, other relevant audiences in the area of operations, and friendly operations. Task execution is evaluated using measures of performance. Task effectiveness is evaluated using measures of effectiveness, which compare achieved results against a baseline. Additional information on assessment and the unique considerations involved in assessing IO are found in chapter 8.

6-23. Based on the IO effects evaluation, the IO officer adjusts IO to further exploit enemy vulnerabilities, redirects actions yielding insufficient effects, or terminates actions after they have achieved the desired result. The IO officer keeps the G-3 (S-3) and commander informed of IO effects and how these impact friendly and adversary operations. Some of the possible changes to IO include:

- Strike a target or continue to protect a critical asset to ensure the desired effect.
- Execute a branch or sequel.

DECISION MAKING DURING EXECUTION

6-24. Decision making during execution includes:

- Executing IO as planned.
- Adjusting IO to a changing friendly situation.
- Adjusting IO to an unexpected enemy reaction.

EXECUTING IO AS PLANNED

6-25. Essential to execution is a continuous information flow among the various functional and integrating cells. The IO officer tracks execution with intelligence and current operations cells, as well as with the targeting staff. The IO officer, in concert with the IO working group, maintains a synchronization matrix. This matrix is periodically updated and provided to the headquarters' functional and integrating cells. Using the matrix, the IO officer and working group keep record of completed IRC tasks. As tasks are completed, the IO officer passes the information to the intelligence cell. The IO officer and working group use this information to keep IO synchronized with the overall operation.

6-26. The IO officer determines whether the threat commander and other identified leaders are reacting to IO as anticipated during course of action analysis. The IO officer, in concert with the IO working group, looks for new threat vulnerabilities and for new IO-related targets. The IO officer proposes changes to the operation order (OPORD) to deal with variances throughout execution. The G-3 (S-3) issues FRAGORDs pertaining to IO, as requested by the IO officer. These FRAGORDs may implement changes to the scheme of IO, IO objectives, and IRC tasks. The IO officer updates the IO synchronization matrix and IO assessment plan to reflect these changes.

6-27. Given the flexibility of advanced information systems, the time available to exploit new threat command and control vulnerabilities may be limited and requires an immediate response from designated IRCs. Actions to defeat threat information efforts need to be undertaken before exploitation advantage disappears. The G-3 (S-3) may issue a verbal FRAGORD when immediate action is required.

ADJUSTING IO TO A CHANGING FRIENDLY SITUATION

6-28. As IO is executed, it often varies from the plan. Possible reasons for a variance include:

- An IO task is aborted or assets redirected.
- An IO-related target did not respond as anticipated.
- The threat effectively countered an IO attack.
- The threat successfully disrupted friendly mission command.
- The initial plan did not identify an emergent IO-related target or target of opportunity.

6-29. The IO officer's challenge is to rapidly assess how changes in IO execution affect the overall operation and to determine necessary follow-on actions. Based on the commander's input, the IO officer, in coordination with the rest of the headquarters' functional and integrating cells, considers COAs, conducts a quick COA analysis, and determines the most feasible COA.

6-30. If the selected COA falls within the decision-making authority of the G-3 (S-3), IO execution can be adjusted without notifying the commander. When changes exceed previously designated limits, the IO officer obtains approval from the commander. At this point, a more formal decision-making process may be required before issuing a FRAGORD, especially if a major adjustment to the operation order (OPORD) is needed. In such a case, the IO officer, working with the G-3 (S-3), participates in a time-constrained military decisionmaking process (MDMP) to develop a new COA.

ADJUSTING IO TO AN UNEXPECTED THREAT REACTION

6-31. The threat may react in an unexpected manner to IO or to the overall operation. If threat actions diverge significantly from those anticipated when the OPORD was written, the commander and staff look first at branch and sequel plans. If branch or sequel plans fail to adequately address the new situation, a new planning effort may be required.

6-32. The IO officer prepares branches that modify defend weighted efforts when threat actions cause new friendly vulnerabilities, or when friendly attack or stabilize efforts prove ineffective. The intelligence and current operations integration cells work with the IO officer to maintain a running assessment of threat capability to disrupt friendly mission command, and look for ways to lessen friendly vulnerabilities. Concurrently, they look for opportunities to reestablish IO effectiveness. Under these conditions, the IO officer determines the adequacy of existing branches and sequels. If none fit the situation, they create a new branch or sequel and disseminate it by FRAGORD.

6-33. If a new plan is needed, time available dictates the length of the decision-making process and the amount of detail contained in an order. The IO officer may only be able to recommend the use of IRCs that can immediately affect the overall operation: for example, electronic warfare, and MISO. Other IRCs proceed as originally planned and are adjusted later, unless they conflict with the new plan.

OTHER EXECUTION CONSIDERATIONS

6-34. Other considerations include, but are not limited to—
- IO execution begins early.
- IO execution requires flexibility.

IO EXECUTION BEGINS EARLY

6-35.   Potential adversary and enemy commanders begin forming perceptions of a situation well before they encounter friendly forces. Recognizing this fact, commanders establish a baseline of IO that is practiced routinely in garrison and training. Selected IRCs (for example, MISO, OPSEC, combat camera, and military deception) begin contributing to an IO objective well before a deployment occurs. To support early execution of the overall operation, IO planning, preparation, and execution frequently begin well before the staff formally starts planning for an operation.

IO EXECUTION REQUIRES FLEXIBILITY

6-36.   Actions by threat decision makers sometimes take surprising turns, uncovering unanticipated weaknesses or strengths. Similarly, friendly commanders may react unexpectedly in response to threat activities. Flexibility is key to success in IO execution. Effective commanders and well-trained staffs are flexible enough to expect the unexpected and exploit threat vulnerabilities/friendly strengths and protect against threat strengths/friendly vulnerabilities.

Other books we publish on Amazon.com

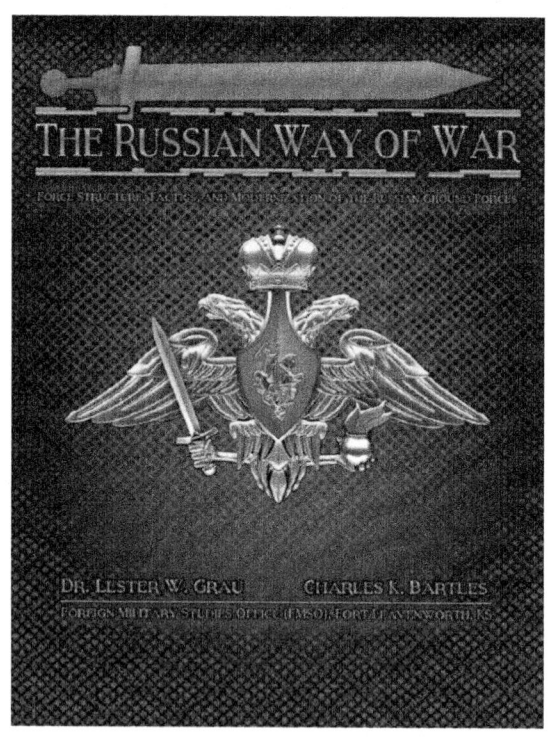

Chapter 7

Targeting Integration

7-1.   Targeting is the process of selecting and prioritizing targets and matching the appropriate response to them, considering operational requirements and capabilities (JP 3-0). IO is integrated into the targeting cycle to produce effects in and through the information environment that support objectives. The targeting cycle facilitates the engagement of the right target with the right asset at the right time. The IO officer or representative is a part of the targeting team, responsible to the commander and staff for all aspects of IO.

TARGETING METHODOLOGY

7-2.   Army targeting methodology is based on four functions: decide, detect, deliver, and assess (D3A) (see Figure 7-1, page 7-2). The decide function occurs concurrently with planning. The detect function occurs during preparation and execution. The deliver function occurs primarily during execution, although some IO-related targets may be engaged while the command is preparing for the overall operation. The assess function occurs throughout.

7-3.   The targeting process is cyclical. The command's battle rhythm determines the frequency of targeting working group meetings. IO-related target nominations are developed by the IO officer and by the IO working group, which validates all IO-related targets before they are nominated to the targeting working group. Therefore, the IO working group is always scheduled in advance of the targeting working group.

DECIDE

7-4.   The decide function is part of the planning activity of the operations process. It occurs concurrently with the military decisionmaking process (MDMP). During the decide function, the targeting team focuses and sets priorities for intelligence collection and attack planning. Based on the commander's intent and concept of operations, the targeting team establishes targeting priorities for each phase or critical event of an operation. The following products reflect these priorities—

- High-payoff target list.
- Information collection plan.
- Target selection standards.
- Attack guidance matrix.
- Target synchronization matrix.

7-5.   The high-payoff target list is a prioritized list of targets whose loss to the enemy will significantly contribute to the success of the friendly course of action. High-payoff targets (HPTs) are those high-value targets (HVTs) identified during COA development and validated in subsequent steps that must be acquired and successfully attacked for the success of the friendly commander's mission. Examples of IO-related HPTs are threat command and control nodes and intelligence collection assets/capabilities.

7-6.   The information collection plan, prepared by the G-3 (S-3) and coordinated with the entire staff, synchronizes the four primary means information collection to provide intelligence to the commander. The G-2 (S-2) ensures all available collection assets provide the required information. Information requirements submitted by the IO officer can require longer lead times to detect targets and dwell times to assess the effects of IRCs directed against these targets.

	Operations Process Activity	Targeting Process Function	Targeting Task

ASSESSMENT	PLANNING	DECIDE	**Mission Analysis**
			Develop IO-related HVTs
			Provide IO input to targeting guidance and targeting objectives
			
			COA Development
			Designate potential IO-related HPTs
			Contribute to the threat and vulnerability assessment
			Deconflict and coordinate potential HPTs
			
			COA Analysis
			Develop high priority target list
			Establish target selection standards
			Develop AGM
			Determine criteria of
			   • Successful BDA
			   • Requirements
			
			Orders Production
			Finalize high-payoff target list
			Finalize target selection standards
			Finalize AGM
			Submit IO information requirements/requests for information to G-2 (S-2)

ASSESSMENT	PREPARATION / EXECUTION	DETECT	• Execute collection plan • Update PIRs/IO IRs as they are answered • Update high-payoff target list and AGM
ASSESSMENT	PREPARATION / EXECUTION	DELIVER	• Execute attacks in accordance with the AGM
ASSESSMENT		ASSESS	• Evaluate effects of attacks • Monitor targets attacked with nonlethal IO

AGM	BDA	COA	HPT	HVT	IO	PIR
attack guidance matrix	battle damage assessment	course of action	high-payoff target	high-value target	Information operations	priority intelligence requirements

Figure 7-1. The operations process, targeting cycle and IO-related tasks

7-7. Target selection standards establish criteria for deciding when targets are located accurately enough to attack. These criteria are often more complicated for IO, especially when attempting to identify actors and audiences with precision.

7-8. The attack guidance matrix addresses how and when targets are to be engaged and desired effects of the engagement. For IO-related targets, effects are diverse, running the gamut from destruction of assets to changed behaviors.

7-9. The target synchronization matrix is a list of HPTs by category and the agencies responsible for detecting them, attacking them, and assessing the effects of the attacks. It combines data from the high-payoff target list, information collection plan and attack guidance matrix.

7-10. The targeting team develops or contributes to these products throughout the MDMP. The commander approves them during COA approval. The IO officer ensures they include information necessary to engage IO-related targets. IO-related vulnerability analyses done by the G-2 (S-2) and IO officer provide a basis for deciding which IO-related targets to attack.

MISSION ANALYSIS

7-11. The two targeting-related IO products of mission analysis are a list of IO-related HVTs and recommendations for the commander's targeting guidance. The IO officer works with the G-2 (S-2) during IPB to develop IO-related HVTs, and with other members of the targeting team to develop IO targeting guidance recommendations.

Intelligence Preparation of the Battlefield

7-12. IPB includes preparing templates that portray threat forces and assets unconstrained by the environment. The intelligence cell adjusts threat templates based on terrain and weather to create situational templates that portray possible threat COAs. These situational templates allow the intelligence to identify HVTs. The IO officer works with the intelligence cell throughout IPB to identify threat information-related capabilities and vulnerabilities and other key groups in the area of operations. These capabilities and vulnerabilities become IO-related HVTs.

Targeting Guidance

7-13. Issued within the commander's guidance is targeting guidance. This guidance describes the desired effects the commander wants to achieve. IO targeting focuses on HVTs that support critical, information-related threat capabilities that underpin their objectives and are vulnerable to friendly IO exploitation.

7-14. The IO officer develops input to targeting guidance based on the initial mission and available and anticipated IRCs. The IO officer identifies the functions, capabilities, or units to be attacked; the effects desired; and the purpose for the attack. The IO officer uses the targeting guidance to select IO-related HPTs from among identified HVTs. These HPTs are confirmed during COA analysis.

7-15. Targeting guidance is developed separately from IO objectives. IO objectives are generally broad in scope. They encompass all IO weighted efforts (attack, defend, stabilize). The IO officer develops recommendations for targeting guidance that supports achieving objectives.

7-16. When developing IO input to the targeting guidance, the IO officer considers the time required to achieve effects and the time required to determine results. Some IRCs require targeting guidance that allows for the acquisition, engagement, and assessment of targets while the unit is preparing for the overall operation. For example, the commander may want to psychologically and electronically isolate the enemy's reserve before engaging it with fires. Doing this requires electronic attack of threat command and control systems and military information support operations (MISO) directed at the threat 24 to 48 hours before lethal fires are initiated. Successfully achieving IO objectives for this phase of the operation requires targeting guidance that gives IO-related targets the appropriate priority.

COURSE OF ACTION DEVELOPMENT

7-17. Feasible COAs, that integrate the effects of all elements of combat power, are developed by the staff. The IO officer prepares a scheme of IO that identifies objectives and IRC tasks for each COA. The IRC tasks are correlated with targets on the HVT list. A single IRC or multiple IRCs can be planned against a single HVT.

7-18. For each COA, the IO officer identifies HVTs that will support attainment of an IO objective. IO-related HVTs that subsequently support friendly IO objectives, and that can be engaged by IRCs, become HPTs. The targeting team also performs target value analysis, coordinates and deconflicts targets, and establishes assessment criteria. The IO officer participates in each of these tasks.

Target Value Analysis

7-19. The targeting team performs target value analysis for each COA the staff develops. The initial sources for target value analysis are target spreadsheets and target sheets. Target spreadsheets (target folders) identify target sets associated with adversary functions that could interfere with each friendly COA or that are key to adversary success. IO-related targets can be analyzed as a separate target set or incorporated into other target sets. The IO officer establishes any IO-specific target sets. Each target set is assigned a priority based on its contribution to the success of a friendly objective, its impact on an enemy or adversary COA, and friendly capability to service the target.

7-20. The targeting team uses target spreadsheets during the war game to determine which HVTs to attack. The IO officer ensures that target spreadsheets include information on threat capabilities and IO-related HVTs and that the IO target set, if designated, is assigned a value appropriate to IO's relative importance to each friendly COA. If an IO target set is not designated, the IO officer ensures that IO-related targets are assigned an appropriate priority within the target sets used.

7-21. Target sheets contain the information required to engage a specific target. Target sheets state how attacking the target affects the threat's operation. The IO officer prepares target sheets for HVTs to analyze them from an IO planning perspective. These HVTs are expressed as target subsets, such as decision makers. Information requirements concerning them include:

- What influences these decision makers.
- How they communicate.
- With whom they communicate.
- Weaknesses, susceptibilities, accessibility, feasibility, and pressure points.

Deconflicting and Coordinating Targets

7-22. The IO officer and working group consider the possible consequences of attacking any target or target set. Their purpose is to identify possible duplication or attenuation of effects. The attack of physical targets always has second- and third-order effects (informational and cognitive) that could diminish or enhance their value to the overall operation. For example, fires that result in the collateral deaths of civilian non-combatants can have a negative cognitive effect, while using fires to destroy the enemy's fiber network so that it relies on radio communications vulnerable to jamming can have a positive informational effect. Also, the effects achieved by one IRC might compete with or diminish the effects of another IRC. Thus, IRC synchronization and the integration of IO into other lines of effort requires methodical coordination and deconfliction efforts.

7-23. IO working group members consider all targets from their various perspectives. Deconfliction in this context means ensuring that engaging a target does not produce effects that interfere with the effects of other IRC tasks or IO-related targets, or otherwise inhibit mission accomplishment. Coordination ensures that the effects of engaging different targets complement each other and further the commander's intent.

7-24. IO officers at different echelons may seek to engage the same targets and, possibly, desire different effects. Therefore, IO-focused targeting includes coordinating and deconflicting targets with higher and subordinate units before the targeting working group meets. Some IO-related targets may also be nominated by other staff elements. The IO officer presents the effects required to accomplish the IO objective associated with those targets when the targeting team determines how to engage them. IO officers must also coordinate and deconflict targets with unified action partners whose doctrinal use of IRCs and policies governing their employment differ. Such coordination extends the planning horizon and may limit how IRCs are integrated.

7-25. One way to achieve this coordination and deconfliction is by beginning parallel planning as early as possible in the MDMP. This means that the IO officer and the targeting team should share all pertinent information with subordinate units and adjacent and higher headquarters.

Assessment Criteria

7-26. Generally, the effects of lethal attacks can be evaluated quickly using readily observable and quantifiable criteria, such as the percentage of the target destroyed. Assessing nonlethal attacks often requires monitoring the target over time, using a mix of quantitative and qualitative criteria. Establishing meaningful measures of performance and effectiveness for IO-related targets requires formulating a theory or logic of change in relation to IO objectives and the desired end state. The IO officer and working group essentially ask: will successful attack of a specific target or target set contribute to the attainment of the objective and what will the observable actions or activities leading to the desired outcome look like? The logic of change is expressed in terms of the anticipated causal chain that begins when the target is engaged. (See chapter 8 for more detail on the theory or logic of change.)

7-27. IO-related targets attacked by means such as jamming or MISO broadcasts require assessment by means other than those used in battle damage assessment. The IO officer develops post-attack or post-engagement assessment criteria for these targets and determines the information needed to determine how well they have been met. The IO officer prepares IO IRs or RFIs for this information. If these targets are approved, the IO IRs for the approved targets may be recommended to the commander as priority intelligence requirements. If the command does not have the assets to answer these IO IRs, the target is not engaged unless the attack guidance specifies otherwise or the commander so directs.

COURSE OF ACTION ANALYSIS

7-28. COA analysis (war-gaming) is a disciplined process that staffs use to visualize the flow of a battle. During the war game, the staff decides or determines—
- Which HVTs are HPTs.
- When to engage each HPT.
- Which system or capability to use against each HPT.
- The desired effects of each attack, expressed in terms of the targeting objectives.
- Which HPTs require battle damage assessment or post-attack/engagement assessment. The IO officer submits IRs for IO-related targets to the G-2 (S-2) for inclusion in the collection plan.
- Which HPTs require special instructions or require coordination.

7-29. Based on the war game, the targeting team produces the following draft targeting products for each COA:
- High-payoff target list.
- Target selection standards.
- Attack guidance matrix.
- Target synchronization matrix.

High-Payoff Target List

7-30. During mission analysis, the IO officer identifies potential targets, which are vetted by the IO working group. The IO officer takes nominated targets to the next targeting working group and works within that body to get these targets onto the high-payoff target list and approved by the targeting board.

Target Selection Standards

7-31. Target selection standards are applied to enemy activities to decide whether the activity can be engaged as a target. Target selection standards are usually disseminated as a matrix. Military intelligence analysts use target selection standards to determine targets from combat information and pass them to fire support assets for attack. Attack systems' managers, such as fire control elements and fire direction centers, use target selection standards to determine whether to attack a potential target. The intelligence and fires cells determine target selection standards. The IO officer ensures that they consider IO-related targets and establish appropriate standards for engaging them.

7-32. For nonlethal attacks or engagements, the IO officer may have to develop descriptive criteria to supplement or replace criteria developed by the fires cell. For example, target selection standards during a security cooperation operation may describe what constitutes a hostile crowd, such as: a group larger than 25 people, armed with sticks or other weapons, and with leaders using radios or cellular telephones to direct it.

Attack Guidance Matrix

7-33. The targeting team recommends attack guidance based on the results of the war game. Attack guidance is normally disseminated as a matrix. An attack guidance matrix includes the following information, listed by target set or HPT:
- Timing of attacks (expressed as immediate, planned, or as acquired).
- Attack system assigned.
- Attack criteria (expressed as neutralize, suppress, harass, or destroy).
- Restrictions or special instructions.

7-34. Only one attack guidance matrix is produced for execution at any point in the operation; however, each phase of the operation may have its own matrix. To synchronize effects, all lethal and nonlethal attack systems, including MISO and electronic attack, for example, are placed on the attack guidance matrix. The attack guidance matrix is a synchronization and integration tool. It is normally included as part of the fire support annex. However, it is not a tasking document. Attack tasks for unit assets, including IRCs, are identified as taskings to subordinate units and agencies in the body or appropriate annexes or appendixes of the OPLAN/ OPORD.

Target Synchronization Matrix

7-35. The target synchronization matrix lists HPTs by category and the agencies responsible for detecting them, attacking them, and assessing the effects of the attacks. It combines data from the high-payoff target list, information collection plan, and attack guidance matrix. A completed target synchronization matrix allows the targeting team to verify that assets have been assigned to each targeting process task for each target. The targeting team may prepare a target synchronization matrix for each COA, or may use the high-payoff target list, target selection standards, and attack guidance matrix for the war game and prepare a target synchronization matrix for only the approved COA.

COURSE OF ACTION COMPARISON AND APPROVAL AND ORDERS PRODUCTION

7-36. After war-gaming all the COAs, the staff compares them and recommends one to the commander for approval. When the commander approves a COA, the targeting products for that COA become the basis for targeting for the operation. The targeting team meets to finalize the high-payoff target list, target selection standards, attack guidance matrix, and input to the information collection plan. The team also performs any additional coordination required. After accomplishing these tasks, targeting team members ensure that targeting factors that fall within their functional areas are placed in the appropriate part of the OPLAN/OPORD.

DETECT

7-37. This function involves locating HPTs accurately enough to engage them. It primarily entails execution of the information collection plan. All staff agencies, including the IO officer, are responsible for passing to the G-2 (S-2) information collected by their assets that answer IRs. Conversely, the G-2 (S-2) is responsible for passing combat information and intelligence to the agencies that identified the IRs. Sharing information allows timely evaluation of attacks, assessment of IO, and development of new targets. Effective information and knowledge management are, therefore, essential.

7-38. The information collection plan focuses on identifying HPTs and answering PIRs. These are prioritized based on the importance of the target or information to the commander's concept of operation and intent. When designated by the commander, PIRs can include requirements concerning IO; obtaining answers to these requirements will assist the IO officer in assessing IO. Thus, there is some overlap between detect and assess functions. Detecting targets for nonlethal attacks may require information collection support from higher headquarters. The targeting team adjusts the high-payoff target list and attack guidance matrix to meet changes as the situation develops. The IO officer submits new IO IRs/RFIs as needed.

7-39. During the detect function, the IO officer updates the high-payoff target list and target synchronization matrix. In addition to the information collection plan, the IO officer will use other information sources, particularly culturally-attuned ones that have unique access to or knowledge of the information environment and its various audiences. Examples include atmospheric teams; cultural attaches or advisors; joint, interorganizational or multinational partner cultural experts; interpreters, or indigenous leaders.

DELIVER

7-40. This function occurs primarily during execution, although some IO-related targets may be engaged while the command is preparing for the overall operation. The key to understanding the deliver function is to know which assets are available to perform a specific function or deliver a specific effect and to ensure these assets are ready and capable. Examples of delivery methods include but are not limited to:

- Corps/division/brigade commander.
- Provincial reconstruction team member or other unified action partner.
- Host nation government leader.

- Loudspeaker.
- Media broadcast.
- Social media posts and videos.
- Patrols.

7-41. During this step, the IO officer executes relevant portions of the target synchronization matrix. As IO-related delivery means and methods are multi-faceted and often involve human interaction, this step includes recording the delivery act and keeping detailed accounts or notes of actions taken or the proceedings, discussions, and commitments involved. The IO officer will ensure that required reporting procedures are explained and disseminated in the operations order or as part of the unit's standard operating procedures.

ASSESS

7-42. There are multiple types and levels of assessment. Assessment within D3A specifically focuses on whether the commander's targeting guidance was met for a specific target. From an IO perspective, such guidance may speak in terms of influence or degraded decision making, which are difficult to quantify. In the case of engagements, for example, assessment will help determine whether messages were retained by the target, whether these messages resulted in changed behavior, and whether reengagement may be necessary. An ongoing consideration in the information environment is that there may be a significant lag between the time of delivery, the effect taking place, and determination of an effect.

7-43. During this step, the IO officer and IRCs evaluate measures of effectiveness and performance to determine if desired effects were achieved. If not, it recommends re-engagement or other actions.

OTHER TARGETING METHODOLOGIES

7-44. The D3A method is employed for deliberate targeting. Other methodologies exist to deal with different mission sets and types of units. They are not meant to replace D3A, but complement it. These other methodologies include:

- Find, fix, track, target, engage, and assess.
- Find, fix, finish, exploit, analyze, and disseminate.

FIND, FIX, TRACK, TARGET, ENGAGE, AND ASSESS

7-45. This methodology is employed primarily for dynamic targeting, which is targeting that prosecutes targets identified too late, or not selected for action in time to be included in deliberate targeting (JP 3-60). An emergent target of opportunity or a change in the situation may necessitate a change to a planned target. These targets still require confirmation, verification, validation, and authorization, but in a shorter timeframe than deliberate targeting allows. Dynamic targeting focuses on time-sensitive targets and HPTs. From an IO perspective, many targets may be time-sensitive. Examples include: a hard-to-reach or inaccessible key leader, a flash mob, an accident requiring combat camera documentation, or a denial-of-service attack or other disruption to communication flow. (See ATP 3-60.1, Appendix A.)

FIND, FIX, FINISH, EXPLOIT, ANALYZE, AND DISSEMINATE

7-46. This methodology is particularly useful in targeting high-value individuals. A high-value individual is a person of interest who is identified, surveilled, tracked, influenced, or engaged. Though typically used by special operations forces, find, fix, finish, exploit, analyze, and disseminate helps maneuver leaders at all levels with aligning intelligence and operations assets for pinpoint targeting of personalities and exploiting vulnerabilities in a given network. (See ATP 3-60, Appendix B).

Other books we publish on Amazon.com

**Fundamentals
Of Tactical
Command and
Control**

A Soviet View

SOVIET MILITARY THOUGHT

Camouflage

A Soviet View

Dictionary
of
Basic Military
Terms

A Soviet View

Tactics

A Soviet View

Soviet Military Thought

Chapter 8

Assessment

8-1. Assessment precedes and guides the other activities of the operations process. It is also part of targeting. In short, assessment occurs at all levels and within all operations and has a role in any process or activity. The purpose of assessment is to improve the commander's decision making and make operations more effective. Assessment is a key component of the commander's decision cycle, helping to determine the results of unit actions in the context of overall mission objectives. Assessment provides information about the current state of the operational environment, the progress of the operation, and recommendations to mitigate or overcome discrepancies between actual and predicted progress. It also reveals how specific capabilities, such as IRCs, contribute to this progress. Commanders adjust operations based on assessment results to ensure objectives are met and the military end state is achieved.

ASSESSMENT PRIORITIZATION

8-2. Assessment has little value unless it meets the needs of its users. It does this by supporting two critical aspects of mission command: shared understanding and decision making. When prioritized and resourced adequately, assessment facilitates a more detailed shared understanding among the commander, staff, and other stakeholders about how the operation is progressing. Regardless of the level or frequency of assessment data collection, staffs will provide the commander ongoing assessment updates.

8-3. Staff assessments, along with those received from higher headquarters or unified action partners, combine with the commander's personal assessment to create an overall assessment, which informs the commander's subsequent decisions. The commander may decide to stay the current course or to issue a FRAGORD to reprioritize missions or tasks, terminate or initiate activities, or redirect resources or the allocation of forces to achieve overall mission objectives. The commander can also direct the development of a new operational approach or plan, if necessary.

8-4. IO contributes to overall operations assessment by examining efforts in and through the information environment. IO-focused assessment is an integral part of the unit's assessment plan, which is discussed broadly in ADRP 5-0 and in detail in FM 6-0. ADRP 5-0 provides overarching guidance on assessment; however, there are unique considerations to the assessment of IO that commanders and staffs take into account.

ASSESSMENT RATIONALE

8-5. Assessment or evaluation is a judgment of merit of an action or operation as to whether it achieved its intended outcome(s). It supports planning, improves effectiveness and efficiency of operations, and enforces accountability. These three purposes correspond to three types of evaluation: formative, process, and summative.

8-6. Formative evaluation supports planning by examining whether an operation or program is being designed to meet its intended purpose. In terms of IO, it involves testing messages, determining baselines, analyzing audiences, and developing the logic by which the operation will create influence.

8-7. Process evaluation occurs primarily during execution and serves to enhance effectiveness and efficiency, as well as facilitate in-process decision making. In terms of IO, it assesses whether the scheme of IO is being executed as planned. If the scheme is not going as planned, process evaluation facilitates decisions that lead to corrective action.

8-8. Summative evaluation occurs post-execution and supports decision making and accountability. While process evaluation supports decisions that adjust activities or efforts as the operation unfolds, summative evaluation supports decisions about the overall operation and whether it achieved the commander's intent. It leads to the determination of those aspects of the operation to sustain and those to eliminate or curtail should a similar operation be undertaken in the future.

8-9. In addition to supporting users such as the IO officer, the IO working group, IRC managers, other staff sections, and the commander, operations assessment feeds higher headquarters assessment and, oftentimes, external entities, such as governmental leadership. IO efforts, in particular, often elicit congressional scrutiny and commander-led assessment ensures units are ready to demonstrate the effectiveness of their influence efforts.

8-10. Assessment is most valuable when operations or operational efforts are not working as planned because it helps the commander and staff figure out why and take corrective action. Units should avoid using assessment to justify decisions already made or merely to check the box. Assessment without the intent to employ its results is a waste of time and resources.

PRINCIPLES THAT ENHANCE THE EFFECTIVENESS OF IO ASSESSMENT

8-11. Assessment effectiveness is enhanced when it adheres to the following principles or best practices:
- Uses clear, realistic and measurable objectives.
- Begins with planning.
- Employs an explicit logic of the effort.
- Is continual and consistent over time.
- Is iterative.
- Is prioritized and resourced.

8-12. Assessment is more effective when IO objectives are specific, measurable, achievable, relevant and time-bound. Creating clear, realistic, and measurable objectives can be challenging early on, as initial guidance from higher might lack clarity. The IO officer asks clarifying questions but also proactively establishes the most specific, measurable, achievable, relevant, and time-bound objectives possible and provides them to higher headquarters for review and refinement. The IO officer also tests its objective statements with relevant stakeholders, most especially the IRCs that contribute to the attainment of these objectives.

8-13. Because IO creates effects in and through the information environment to influence, disrupt, corrupt, or usurp threat and other audience behavior and decision making, it is necessary to understand what the desired behavior looks like. This understanding drives the planning necessary to achieve the desired outcome. In other words, effective planning for IO cannot occur unless assessment is part of the operations process from the beginning.

8-14. Unlike fires, whose effects are rapidly discernable, effects in the information environment may not be immediate and their causality can be difficult to determine. An essential part of planning and assessing IO is the need to develop an explicit logic of the effort for each objective or effect. The logic of the effort makes explicit how specific efforts lead to the attainment of objectives. The value of this logic is that its assumptions are made explicit and can become hypotheses that can then be tested and, if necessary, refined. Figure 8-1 on page 8-3 provides a simple example of a logic statement and how it evolves when its hypothesis is tested. More complex examples would include additional threat counter-measures that would test each successive hypothesis and the refinement of the IRC mix necessary to create as foolproof a logic as possible, balanced against risk, available assets, time, and cost.

8-15. Since IO objectives are primarily articulated in terms of a change in one (or more) dimensions of the information environment, a baseline is required to assess progress toward or attainment of the objective. A baseline captures the current state of a person, place, or thing.

8-16. Because evaluation is essential to planning, operational effectiveness and efficiency, and decision making and accountability, it is continual. More important for IO assessment is the fact that objectives are often measured in terms of patterns or trends in behavior. If assessment is not continual and consistent, these patterns or trends become difficult or impossible to detect and measure.

8-17. IO assessment is iterative because, in most instances, IO is iterative. Rarely does a single capability produce a singular and decisive effect that is readily and fully measurable. Effects in the information environment take time to unfold and become fully visible. Indicators are used to show progress towards the desired cumulative outcome, but because progress takes time, things change. The environment changes, the logic of change changes, and the indicators of progress change. In the face of these changes, measures are iteratively refined, corrected and reapplied.

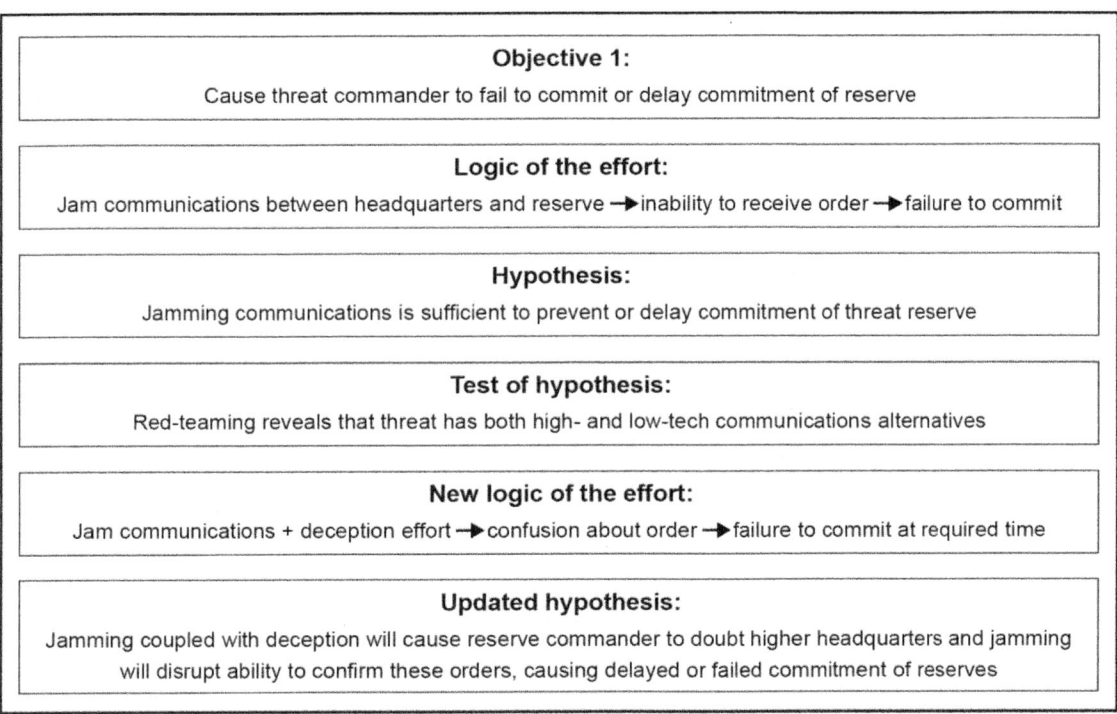

Objective 1:
Cause threat commander to fail to commit or delay commitment of reserve

Logic of the effort:
Jam communications between headquarters and reserve → inability to receive order → failure to commit

Hypothesis:
Jamming communications is sufficient to prevent or delay commitment of threat reserve

Test of hypothesis:
Red-teaming reveals that threat has both high- and low-tech communications alternatives

New logic of the effort:
Jam communications + deception effort → confusion about order → failure to commit at required time

Updated hypothesis:
Jamming coupled with deception will cause reserve commander to doubt higher headquarters and jamming will disrupt ability to confirm these orders, causing delayed or failed commitment of reserves

Figure 8-1. Logic of the effort example

8-18. To be effective, assessment requires commander emphasis, prioritization, and allocation of resources. This requirement does not mean that every activity, event, or operation requires an equal investment in or level of assessment. Through their guidance and direction, commanders make clear their assessment priorities and ensure that IO assessment receives due emphasis and support.

IO ASSESSMENT CONSIDERATIONS

8-19. Assessment of IO in general and of specific effects in the information environment require careful development of measures of effectiveness and performance, as well as identification of indicators that will best signal achievement of these measures and desired outcomes. Assessment in the information environment is not easy and adherence to the following considerations will aid in making IO assessment more effective.

MEASURES OF EFFECTIVENESS

8-20. A *measure of effectiveness* is a criterion used to assess changes in system behavior, capability, or operational environment that is tied to measuring the attainment of an end state, achievement of an objective, or creation of an effect (JP 3-0). Measures of effectiveness help measure changes in conditions, both positive and negative. They are commonly found and tracked in formal assessment plans.

8-21. Time is a factor when assessing IO and developing measures of effectiveness. The attainment of IO objectives leading to the commander's desired end state often requires days or months to realize. It is essential, therefore, to have a baseline from which to measure change and also to time-bound the change. Time-bounding makes clear how long it will take before the change is observed. It helps to set necessary expectations, foster patience, and avoid a rush to judgment. If a behavioral objective is anticipated to take considerable time, assessment planning may choose to break the objective into smaller increments, each with more immediate observable outcomes. Finally, it is also important to analyze and understand the cultural relevance of time in the area of operations and account for and adapt to it.

8-22. Developing informational, behavioral and sentiment baselines often requires significant time and resource investments. Sentiment baselines, such as those determined through surveys or interviews, may require contracted labor to accomplish. The IO officer must factor in the lead time necessary to contract a third-party, provide it time to develop the survey instrument, administer the survey, and tabulate and report on the results.

8-23. Commanders and staffs, particularly the IO officer, must account for the order of effects when assessing IO or, more broadly, any effect. For example, an effect in the physical dimension (1st order) can resonate in unexpected ways in the informational and cognitive dimensions (2nd and 3rd orders). During Operation Enduring Freedom, night raids, while operationally necessary to root out insurgents, caused significant backlash among the indigenous population, local leaders, and the national government. Part of the IO officer's task is to anticipate second- and third-order effects and conduct a risk analysis to determine if potential higher-order effects outweigh the benefits of achieving lower-order effects. The aim is to amplify intended consequences in all dimensions of the information environment, while mitigating unintended consequences.

8-24. Units must account for directness of effect and understand the difference between causational linkages and correlational ones. Certain effects, even desired ones, may not be directly tied to friendly efforts in the information environment; however, friendly forces may still be held accountable for these effects and must react appropriately. This fact underlines the importance of developing a logic of the effort for each IO objective. This logic explicitly states how synchronized IRCs will lead to the desired change expressed in the objective. The logic also differentiates planned activities from other possible contributing factors and articulates expected outputs and outcomes.

8-25. Effectiveness in the cognitive dimension typically requires variety and repetition. Rarely does a single tactic, task, method, action, or message change behavior. Assessment plans must therefore build in varied actions and repeated messages and measure their cumulative effect.

MEASURES OF PERFORMANCE

8-26. A *measure of performance* is a criterion used to assess friendly actions that is tied to measuring task accomplishment (JP 3-0). Measures of performance help answer questions such as "Was the action taken?" or "Were the tasks completed to standard?" A measure of performance confirms or denies that a task has been properly performed. Measures of performance are commonly found and tracked at all echelons in execution matrixes. They are also commonly used to evaluate training.

8-27. There is no definitive number of tasks to support a given objective; therefore, there is no definitive number of measures of performance to support any given measure of effectiveness. Again, variety and repetition necessitate that multiple tasks typically support each objective and the corresponding measure of performance is the means to confirm or deny that each task is executed in the first place and properly performed.

8-28. Delivery, especially means of delivery, is a critical consideration when developing IRC tasks and their associated measures of performance, particularly when it comes to message delivery. No matter how well-crafted the message, if delivery assets are unavailable or only available in insufficient number, the objective will likely not be achieved. Means of delivery should also be considered in terms of accessibility and acceptability to the target audience. For example, if only a small percentage of the population listens to radio or watches television then these means should not be the only means of delivery considered.

INDICATORS

8-29. An *indicator* is an item of information that provides insight into a measure of effectiveness or measure of performance (ADRP 5-0). Indicators take the form of reports from subordinates, surveys and polls, and information requirements. Indicators help to answer the question "What is the current status of this measure of effectiveness?" A single indicator can inform multiple measures of effectiveness.

8-30. Not everything observed is an indicator and not every indicator is a sign of progress. Indicators of psychological effects or changes in sentiment are not always easy to detect or may not be markers of the desired behavior change. The upshot of these facts is that establishing indicators requires rigorous effort in order to select those observable and measurable signs or signals that are reflective of changed behavior. Often behavior change is incremental and being able to detect the intervening steps to large-scale behavior change is essential to measuring progress. Again, in-depth knowledge is required of those targets or audiences for whom behavior change is required to achieve the commander's desired end state.

8-31. Measuring progress requires the ability to detect both micro and macro indicators simultaneously. The IO officer must, therefore, coordinate with the G-2 (S-2) in order to know what collection assets are available and the types of information that each provides and how this information helps create actionable knowledge. Soldiers are a vital collection asset. The IO officer should invest time to train all Soldiers on observation techniques that enable them to spot and discriminate meaningful indicators and ways to report what they see.

8-32. The IO officer should employ a variety of means to identify indicators, validate or corroborate conclusions about them, and measure progress. Some of the more commonly used sources are:

- Information collection assets
- Military Information Support Operations (MISO) teams
- Soldier and leader engagements
- Civil-military operations
- Polling and surveys (which primarily measure attitudes, not motivations)
- Media monitoring and analysis
- Patrol and spot reports
- Information sharing with unified action partners
- Conversations with local leaders, partners, and trusted agents
- Passive monitoring (atmospherics)

8-33. Figure 8-2 portrays the relationship between objectives (the change that needs to happen) and measures of performance, indicators, and measures of effectiveness. The logic of the effort is shown as a relationship between available, selected, and synchronized IRCs and the effects expected over time. While the figure suggests that this logic is generic, it is not. It is unique to every objective and combination of IRCs.

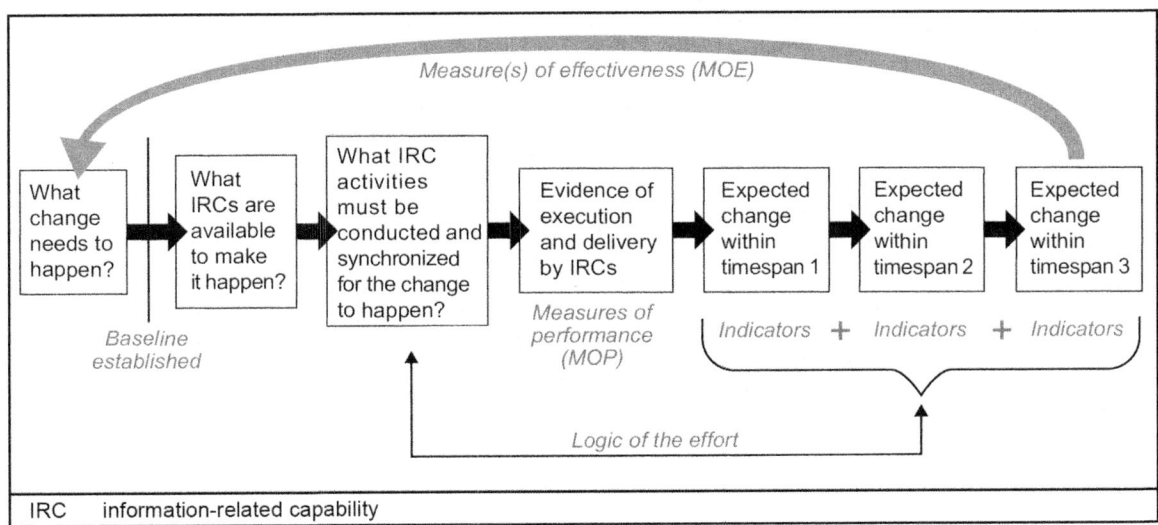

Figure 8-2. Logic flow and components of an IO objective

Other books we publish on Amazon.com

FM 7-22
HOLISTIC HEALTH AND FITNESS

OCT 2020
HEADQUARTERS, DEPARTMENT OF THE ARMY

ATP 7-22.02
HOLISTIC HEALTH AND
FITNESS DRILLS AND
EXERCISES

OCT 2020
HEADQUARTERS, DEPARTMENT OF THE ARMY

ATP 7-22.01
HOLISTIC HEALTH AND FITNESS
TESTING

OCT 2020
HEADQUARTERS, DEPARTMENT OF THE ARMY

ATP 4-02.55
ARMY HEALTH SYSTEM
SUPPORT PLANNING

MARCH 2020
HEADQUARTERS, DEPARTMENT OF THE ARMY

Chapter 9

Brigade and Below Information Operations

9-1.   IO integration and synchronization activities are essential to mission success at all levels. At brigade and below, units synchronize fewer IRCs but their effects are more immediate and, proportionately, more integral to achieving unit objectives. Brigade and below and especially small-unit operations require Soldiers to be ready and capable of effectively engaging the local populace while part of patrols, convoys, and tactical actions. Brigade and below operations also take advantage of effects being achieved by IRCs at higher levels and makes them relevant to a unit's area of operations.

9-2.   As an example, IO considerations during patrols expand the purpose of patrols beyond combat operations and reconnaissance. Patrols always create effects in the information environment. In addition to gathering information, patrols can execute psychological actions, deliver messages, disseminate information, and influence target audiences through presence and direct interaction. Lower-echelon units must therefore shape this presence to reinforce the commander's intent. Their presence is further shaped and amplified through the use of available higher-echelon IRCs, such as military information support operations (MISO), public affairs, and civil affairs operations. Individual Soldiers must be able to engage the local population and deliver messages in such a way that they influence target and audience behavior in accordance with objectives.

PRESENCE, PROFILE, AND POSTURE

9-3.   Presence, profile and posture are interrelated terms that define and describe a unit's visual, aural, and oral presentation to others. Everything a unit or Soldier does speaks, in some manner, to those who witness or hear it. Presence, profile and posture are an active means by which units can shape sentiments through physical, visual, and audible actions.

PRESENCE

9-4.   Presence, the act of being physically present, always sends a message. Presence can be menacing or reassuring, depending on the situation. Absence, or the lack of presence, can create perceptions that work for or against the unit's aims. Being very conscious and deliberate about being present or absent can be a powerful form of influence and should not be left to chance. Once units determine that presence is required, or that there is no choice but to be present, how they convey that presence is important. Both profile and posture address the way that units, patrols, and Soldiers are present.

PROFILE

9-5.   Profile is about the degree of presence, both in terms of quantity and quality. Quantity is reflected in how much a unit is present, as in its footprint or task organization. Quality speaks to the nature of that presence, as in its current capability, as well as its reputation.

9-6.   During the conduct of offensive- and defensive-focused operations, a unit tends to optimize its profile, not simply in number of forces but in terms of all assets or effects it can bring to bear. Here is where an information-related capability (IRC) like military deception can play a significant role. It allows commanders to make their force appear larger or more substantial than it is. In contrast, during stability-focused operations, the aim is often to keep one's profile to a minimum—to conduct an operation with the smallest force necessary to ensure force protection but not appear unduly threatening. Therefore, a unit's profile may be both minimized and optimized through partnership efforts with local national security forces.

9-7.   Quality of presence significantly affects perceptions or sentiments, either positively or negatively, and requires continual vigilance. Soldiers and leaders must be conscious of their personal profile and actively work to build and preserve their credibility.

POSTURE

9-8.   Posture is an expression of attitude. Whether active or passive, threatening or non-threatening, or defensive or welcoming. Posture dictates how units or Soldiers appear to others and how they act towards them.

9-9.   Posture is determined by the operational environment and necessity. For example, if force protection is paramount, a unit might decide to wear full protection and appear more aggressive in its stance and movements. If persuading the local population to support an upcoming change to the way biometrics are gathered is paramount, a unit might decide to wear soft hats and no body armor.

9-10. The relationship between posture and profile enables one to counterbalance the other. A unit at a numerical disadvantage can compensate through an aggressive posture. Conversely, a unit with more than enough forces can soften its posture, appropriate to the situation.

SOLDIER AND LEADER ENGAGEMENTS

9-11. Like presence, profile and posture, Soldier and leader engagement (SLE) is an IRC that every unit inherently has at its disposal and for which it is responsible to employ. Patrols conduct deliberate SLE as part of their mission but must be ready to conduct dynamic SLEs; that is, unplanned engagements with local audiences with whom they come in contact during the routine conduct of the patrol. While these interactions may be impromptu, they still benefit from prior planning and training. Themes, messages, and talking points provide Soldiers with the necessary guidance to communicate with target audiences, whether deliberately engaged or inadvertently encountered.

9-12. Planning for dynamic SLEs is integral to planning the patrol. It involves anticipating individuals and groups that the patrol might encounter and developing appropriate response scenarios. Further, it involves reviewing and, to the extent necessary, memorizing the commander's intent, desired end state and narrative, and the messages and talking points that support them. Perhaps most important of all, it means having Soldiers rehearse the response scenarios to a point where they can engage local foreign audiences with confidence, competence, and nuance.

LEVERAGING OTHER IRCS

9-13. At the brigade level, the S3 coordinates with IRC experts and other members on the staff to support tactical-level operations and produce desired effects in and through the information environment. These capabilities are generally requested through the target nomination process and coordinated with the higher headquarters. Common IRCs include, but are not limited to:

* MISO.
* Civil Affairs Operations.
* Combat Camera.
* Electronic Warfare.
* Space Operations.
* Cyberspace operations.
* Military Deception.
* Special Technical Operations.

MILITARY INFORMATION SUPPORT OPERATIONS (MISO)

9-14. A MISO detachment typically supports a brigade combat team. The detachment commander and non-commissioned officer in charge serve on the brigade combat team staff as planners and coordinators of influence activities. They employ subordinate tactical teams to conduct engagement activities, execute psychological actions, deliver messages, use loudspeakers for message delivery and tactical military deception, and for collecting information on the operational environment. Product development and production is a company-level and above function and requires coordination for dedicated support or tailored messages and are subject to applicable or required authorities within the given area of operations.

CIVIL AFFAIRS OPERATIONS

9-15. When planning a patrol, consideration must be given to civil affairs operations that may be ongoing or recently completed in the area that the patrol will occur. Spotlighting or reinforcing these operations, whether through talking points or by presence at the project site, can help reinforce their benefits.

9-16. Civil affairs operations units often develop novelty items that resonate with indigenous audiences, such as school supplies, radios, and sports equipment or apparel. Patrols can employ these items to increase the effects of their engagements and interactions favorably. Commanders can facilitate the development and use of these items by providing access to funding sources and implementing streamlined approval processes. However, these items simply provide the venue to engage an audience and deliver the desired message. They are not the sole purpose of Soldier and leader engagements.

COMBAT CAMERA

9-17. Combat camera provides several benefits to patrols. First, combat camera can record engagements for historical purposes. Second, combat camera images can be used for future public affairs or MISO products. They can also be used to counter threat propaganda. If combat camera assets are not available, units can designate one or more Soldiers to use unit-issued or personal cameras; however, the unit must have a procedure in place for the review, clearance, and disposition of any images taken.

TECHNICAL AND SPECIAL CAPABILITIES

9-18. Electronic warfare assets can be coordinated to support operations by jamming, broadcasting, or spoofing to gain information environment effects that support and reinforce maneuver actions. Space assets can be requested to assist with reconnaissance, surveillance, communications, and imagery support. Requests for assets may have to go through the S-2 or S-6, depending on the specific capability and its intended use.

9-19. Tactical military deceptions can be employed to influence a threat decision maker to take actions that give the friendly force a position of relative advantage. Special technical operations can be employed to create effects within the unit's area of operations that cannot be accomplished by available assets or that would cause too great a risk. Effects in cyberspace may be requested to protect, exploit, or deny the threat the ability to collect or disseminate information in and through cyberspace.

Other books we publish on Amazon.com

Appendix A
IO Input to Operation Plans and Orders

A-1. Commanders and staffs use Appendix 15 (Information Operations) to Annex C (Operations) to operation plans and orders to describe how information operations (IO) will support operations described in the base plan or order. The IO officer is the staff officer responsible for this appendix.

A-2. The Appendix 15 (Figure A-1) that appears on pages A-2 through A-4 is a guide and should not limit the information contained in an actual Appendix 15. Appendix 15 should be specific to the operation being conducted; thus, the content of actual Appendix 15s will vary greatly.

[CLASSIFICATION]

Place the classification at the top and bottom of every page of the OPLAN or OPORD. Place the classification marking at the front of each paragraph and subparagraph in parentheses. See AR 380-5 for classification and release marking instruction.

Copy ## of ## copies
Issuing headquarters
Place of issue
Date-time group of signature
Message reference number

Include heading if attachment is distributed separately from the base order or higher-level attachment.

APPENDIX 15 (INFORMATION OPERATIONS) TO ANNEX C (OPERATIONS) TO OPERATION PLAN/ORDER [number] [(code name)] — [issuing headquarters] [(classification of title)]

(U) **References:** *Refer to higher headquarters' OPLAN or OPORD and identify map sheets for operation (optional). Add any other specific references to IO, if needed.*

1. (U) **Situation.** *Include information affecting information operations (IO) that paragraph 1 of the OPLAN or OPORD does not cover or that needs expansion.*

    a. (U) Area of Interest. *Describe the information environment as it relates to IO. Refer to Tab 1 (Combined Information Overlay) to Appendix 15 (Information Operations) to Annex C (Operations) as required.*

    b. (U) Area of Operations. *Refer to Appendix 2 (Operation Overlay) to Annex C (Operations).*

    (1) (U) Information Environment. *Describe the physical, informational, and cognitive dimensions of the information environment that affect IO. Refer to Tab 1 (Combined Information Overlay) to Appendix 15 (Information Operations) to Annex C (Operations) as required.*

    (2) (U) Weather. *Describe aspects of weather that impact information operations. Refer to Annex B (Intelligence) as required.*

    c. (U) Enemy Forces. *List known and templated locations and activities of enemy information units for one echelon up and two echelons down. List enemy maneuver and information-related capabilities that will impact friendly operations. State probable enemy courses of action and employment of enemy information assets. Describe the informational and cognitive dimensions of the information environment that affect enemy actions. Refer to Tab 1 (Combined Information Overlay) to Appendix 15 (Information Operations) to Annex C (Operations) as required.*

    d. (U) Friendly Forces. *Outline the higher headquarters' plan as it pertains to IO. List designation, location, and outline of plan of higher, adjacent, and other functional area assets that support or impact the issuing headquarters or require coordination and additional support. Identify friendly IO/IRC assets and resources that affect subordinate commander IO planning. Identify friendly forces IO vulnerabilities. Identify friendly foreign forces with which subordinate commanders may operate. Identify potential conflicts within the information environment, especially if conducting joint or multinational operations. Identify and deconflict IRC employment and information environment effects.*

    e. (U) Interagency, Intergovernmental, and Nongovernmental Organizations. *Identify and describe other organizations in the area of operations that may impact the conduct of IO or implementation of IO-specific equipment and tactics.*

    f. (U) Civil Considerations. *Describe critical aspects of the civil situation that impact IO. See Tab C (Civil Considerations) to Appendix 1 (Intelligence Estimate) to Annex B (Intelligence) and Annex K (Civil Affairs Operations) as required. Also refer to Tab 1 (Combined Information Overlay) to Appendix 15 (Information Operations) to Annex C (Operations) as required.*

[page number]
[CLASSIFICATION]

Figure A-1. Appendix 15 (IO) to Annex C (Operations)

[CLASSIFICATION]
APPENDIX 15 (INFORMATION OPERATIONS) TO ANNEX C (OPERATIONS) TO OPERATION PLAN/ORDER [number] [(code name)] — [issuing headquarters] [(classification of title)]

g. (U) <u>Attachments and Detachments</u>. *List IRCs or IO units only as necessary to clarify task organization. Examples include Tactical MISO Teams, Mobile Public Affairs Detachments, and Visual Information Teams. Refer to Annex A (Task Organization) as required.*

h. (U) <u>Assumptions</u>. *List any IO-specific assumptions.*

2. (U) Mission. *State the IO mission.*

3. (U) Execution.

a. (U) <u>Scheme of Support</u>. *Describe how IO supports the commander's intent and concept of operations. Establish the priorities of support to units for each phase of the operation. Establish IO objectives to employ IRCs to achieve the desired endstate. Describe how IO weighted efforts will support offense, defense, and stability tasks. Identify target sets and effects, by priority. Describe the general concept for the integration of IO. List the staff sections, elements, and working groups responsible for aspects of IO. Include IO collection methods for information developed in staff sections, elements, and working groups outside the IO element and working group. Ensure subordinate units and higher headquarters receive the IO synchronization plan. Describe the plan for the integration of unified action and nongovernmental partners and organizations. Refer to Annex C (Operations) as required. This section is designed to provide insight and understanding of how IO is integrated across the operational plan.*

b. (U) <u>Assessment</u>. *Describe the priorities for assessment and identify the measures of performance and effectiveness and indicators used to assess information operations objectives against end state conditions. Refer to Annex M (Assessment) as required.*

c. (U) <u>Tasks to Subordinate Units</u>. *List IO tasks assigned to specific subordinate units not contained in the base order.*

d. (U) <u>Coordinating Instructions</u>. *List only IO instructions applicable to two or more subordinate units not covered in the base order. Identify and highlight any IO-specific rules of engagement, risk reduction control measures, environmental considerations, coordination requirements between units, and CCIRs and EEFIs that pertain to IO.*

4. (U) Sustainment. *Identify priorities of sustainment for IO key tasks and specify additional instructions as required. Refer to Annex F (Sustainment) as required.*

a. (U) <u>Logistics</u>. *Use subparagraphs to identify priorities and specific instruction for logistics pertaining to IO. See Appendix 1 (Logistics) to Annex F (Sustainment) and Annex P (Host-Nation Support) as required.*

b. (U) <u>Personnel</u>. *Use subparagraphs to identify priorities and specific instruction for human resources support pertaining to IO. See Appendix 2 (Personnel Services Support) to Annex F (Sustainment) as required.*

c. (U) <u>Health System Support</u>. *See Appendix 3 (Army Health System Support) to Annex F (Sustainment) as required.*

5. (U) Command and Signal.

a. (U) Command.

(1) (U) <u>Location of Commander</u>. *State the location of key IO leaders.*

(2) (U) <u>Liaison Requirements</u>. *State the IO liaison requirements not covered in the unit's SOPs.*

[page number]
[CLASSIFICATION]

Figure A-1. Appendix 15 (IO) to Annex C (Operations) (continued)

[CLASSIFICATION]
APPENDIX 15 (INFORMATION OPERATIONS) TO ANNEX C (OPERATIONS) TO OPERATION
PLAN/ORDER [number] [(code name)] — [issuing headquarters] [(classification of title)]

b. (U) <u>Control</u>.

(1) (U) <u>Command Posts</u>. *Describe IO integration into command posts (CPs), including the location of each CP and its time of opening and closing.*

(2) (U) <u>Reports</u>. *List IO-specific reports not covered in SOPs. See Annex R (Reports) as required.*

c. (U) <u>Signal</u>. *Address any IO-specific communications requirements. See Annex H (Signal) as required.*

ACKNOWLEDGE: *Include only if attachment is distributed separately from the base order.*

[Commander's last name]
[Commander's rank]

The commander or authorized representative signs the original copy of the attachment. If the representative signs the original, add the phrase "For the Commander." The signed copy is the historical copy and remains in the headquarters' files.

OFFICIAL:
[Authenticator's name]
[Authenticator's position]

Use only if the commander does not sign the original attachment. If the commander signs the original, no further authentication is required. If the commander does not sign, the signature of the preparing staff officer requires authentication and only the last name and rank of the commander appear in the signature block.

ATTACHMENT: List lower-level attachments (tabs and exhibits).
Tab A–Combined Information Overlay
Tab B- Information-Related Capabilities Synchronization Matrix
Tab C–Presence, Posture, and Profile
Tab D–Combat Camera
Tab E–Soldier and Leader Engagement

DISTRIBUTION: *Show only if distributed separately from the base order or higher-level attachments.*

[page number]
[CLASSIFICATION]

Figure A-1. Appendix 15 (IO) to Annex C (Operations) (continued)

Glossary

SECTION I – ACRONYMS AND ABBREVIATIONS

AGM	Attack guidance matrix
C2	command and control
CCIRs	commander's critical information requirements
CO	cyberspace operations
COA	course of action
CP	command post
D3A	decide, detect, deliver, and assess
EEFI	essential elements of friendly information
EW	electronic warfare
FRAGORD	fragmentary order
G-1	assistant chief of staff, personnel
G-2	assistant chief of staff, intelligence
G-3	assistant chief of staff, operations
G-4	assistant chief of staff, logistics
G-5	assistant chief of staff, plans
G-6	assistant chief of staff, signal
G-9	assistant chief of staff, civil affairs operations
HPT	high-payoff target
HVT	high-value target
IPB	intelligence preparation of the battlefield
IO	information operations
IR	information requirement
IRC	information-related capability
MDMP	military decisionmaking process
MISO	military information support operations
OPLAN	operation plan
OPORD	operation order
OPSEC	operations security
PSYOP	psychological operations
WARNORD	warning order

SECTION II – TERMS

combat power

(Army) The total means of destructive, constructive, and information capabilities that a military unit or formation can apply at a given time. (ADRP 3-0)

commander's communication synchronization

A process to coordinate and synchronize narratives, themes, messages, images, operations, and actions to ensure their integrity and consistency to the lowest tactical level across all relevant communication activities. Also called CCS. (JP 3-61)

commander's critical information requirement

An information requirement identified by the commander as being critical to facilitating timely decision making. Also called CCIR. (JP 3-0)

commander's intent

A clear and concise expression of the purpose of the operation and the desired military end state that supports mission command, provides focus to the staff, and helps subordinate and supporting commanders act to achieve the commander's desired results without further orders, even when the operation does not unfold as planned. (JP 3-0)

concept of operations

(Army) A statement that directs the manner in which subordinate units cooperate to accomplish that mission and establish the sequence of actions the force will use to achieve the end state. (ADRP 5-0)

cyberspace

A global domain within the information environment consisting of the interdependent networks of information technology infrastructures and resident data, including the Internet, telecommunications networks, computer systems, and embedded processors and controllers. (JP 3-12)

cyberspace operations

The employment of cyberspace capabilities where the primary purpose is to achieve objectives in or through cyberspace. Also called CO. (JP 3-0)

decisive action

The continuous, simultaneous combinations of offensive, defensive, and stability or defense support of civil authorities tasks. (ADRP 3-0)

end state

The set of required conditions that defines achievement of the commander's objectives. (JP 3-0)

essential element of friendly information

(Army) A critical aspect of a friendly operation that, if known by the enemy, would subsequently compromise, lead to failure, or limit success of the operation and therefore should be protected from enemy detection. Also called EEFI. (ADRP 5-0)

indicator

(Army) In the context of assessment, an item of information that provides insight into a measure of effectiveness or measure of performance. (ADRP 5-0)

information environment

The aggregate of individuals, organizations, and systems that collect, process, dissseminate, or act on information. (JP 3-13)

*information fratricide

Adverse effects on the information environment resulting from a failure to effectively synchronize the employment of multiple information-related capabilities which may impede the conduct of friendly operations or adversely affect friendly forces.

information operations

The integrated employment, during military operations, of information-related capabilities in concert with other lines of operation to influence, disrupt, corrupt, or usurp the decision-making of adversaries and potential adversaries while protecting our own. Also called IO. (JP 3-13)

information-related capability

A tool, technique, or activity employed within a dimension of the information environment that can be used to create effects and operationally desirable conditions. Also called IRC. (JP 3-13).

line of effort

(Army) A line that links multiple tasks using the logic of purpose rather than geographical reference to focus efforts toward establishing operational and strategic conditions. Also called LOE. (ADRP 3-0)

line of operations

(Army) A line that defines the directional orientation of a force in time and space in relation to the enemy and links the force with its base of operations and objectives. (ADRP 3-0)

measure of effectiveness

(DOD) A criterion used to assess changes in system behavior, capability, or operational environment that is tied to measuring the attainment of an end state, achievement of an objective, or creation of an effect. Also called MOE. (JP 3-0)

measure of performance

(DOD) A criterion used to assess friendly actions that is tied to measuring task accomplishment. Also called MOP. (JP 3-0)

message

A narrowly focused communication directed at a specific audience to support a specific theme. Also called MSG. (JP 3-61)

military deception

Actions executed to deliberately mislead adversary military, paramilitary, or violent extremist organization decision makers, thereby causing the adversary to take specific actions (or inactions) that will contribute to the accomplishment of the friendly mission. (JP 3-13.4)

mission command

(Army) The exercise of authority and direction by the commander using mission orders to enable disciplined initiative within the commander's intent to empower agile and adaptive leaders in the conduct of unified land operations. (ADP 6-0)

narrative

Overarching expression of context and desired results. (JDN 2-13)

operational environment

A composite of the conditions, circumstances, and influences that affect the employment of capabilities and bear on the decisions of the commander. Also called OE. (JP 3-0)

planning

The art and science of understanding a situation, envisioning a desired future, and laying out effective ways of bringing that future about. (ADP 5-0)

running estimate

The continuous assessment of the current situation used to determine if the current operation is proceeding according to the commander's intent and if planned future operations are supportable. (ADP 5-0)

*Soldier and leader engagement

Interpersonal Service-member interactions with audiences in an area of operations. Also called SLE.

targeting

(DOD) The process of selecting and prioritizing targets and matching the appropriate response to them, considering operational requirements and capabilities. (JP 3-0)

terrain management

The process of allocating terrain by establishing areas of operation, designating assembly areas, and specifying locations for units and activities to deconflict activities that might interfere with each other. (ADRP 5-0)

theme

Unifying idea or intention that supports the narrative and is designed for broad application to achieve specific objectives. (JDN 2-13)

References

All URLs accessed on 9 September 2016.

REQUIRED PUBLICATIONS

These documents must be available to intended users of this publication.

Department of Defense Dictionary of Military and Associated Terms. 15 October 2016.

ADRP 1-02. *Terms and Military Symbols.* 16 November 2016.

RELATED PUBLICATIONS

These documents contain relevant supplemental information.

JOINT PUBLICATIONS

Most joint publications are available online: http://www.dtic.mil/doctrine/new_pubs/jointpub.htm

JDN 2-13. *Commander's Communication Synchronization.* 16 December 2013.

JP 3-0. *Joint Operations.* 11 August 2011.

JP 3-12. *Cyberspace Operations.* 5 February 2013. This publication is available at
https://jdeis.js.mil/jdeis/index.jsp?pindex=2

JP 3-13. *Information Operations.* 27 November 2012.

JP 3-13.4. *Military Deception.* 26 January 2012.

JP 5-0. *Joint Operation Planning.* 11 August 2011.

JP 3-60. *Joint Targeting.* 31 January 2013

JP 3-61. *Public Affairs.* 17 November 2015.

ARMY PUBLICATIONS

Most Army doctrinal publications are available online: http://armypubs.army.mil/

ADP 5-0. *The Operations Process.* 17 May 2012.

ADP 6-0. *Mission Command.* 17 May 2012.

ADRP 3-0. *Unified Land Operations.* 16 May 2012.

ADRP 5-0. *The Operations Process.* 17 May 2012.

AR 350-2. *Operational Environment and Opposing Force Program.* 19 May 2015.

AR 380-5.*Department of the Army Information Security Program.* 29 September 2000.

ATP 2-01.3. *Intelligence Preparation of the Battlefield.* 10 November 2014.

ATP 3-60. *Targeting.* 7 May 2015.

ATP 3-60.1. *Dynamic Targeting, Multi-Service Tactics, Techniques, and Procedures for Dynamic
Targeting.* {MCRP 3-16D; NTTP 3-60.1; AFTTP 3-2.3} 10 September 2015.

ATP 3-90.1. *Armor and Mechanized Infantry Company Team.* 27 January 2016.

ATP 3-90.37. *Countering Improvised Explosive Devices.* 29 July 2014.

ATP 5-0.1. *Army Design Methodology.* 1 July 2015.

ATP 5-19. *Risk Management.* 14 April 2014.

FM 6-0. *Commander and Staff Organization and Operations.* 5 May 2014.

FM 27-10. *The Law of Land Warfare.* 18 July 1956.

RECOMMENDED READINGS

ADP 3-0 *Unified Land Operations*. 10 October 2011.

ADRP 6-0. *Mission Command*. 17 May 2012.

FM 6-02. *Signal Support to Operations*. 22 January 2014.

FM 7-100.1. *Opposing Force Operations*. 27 December 2004.

TC 7-100. *Hybrid Threat*. 26 November 2010.

TC 7-100.2. *Opposing Force Tactics*. 9 December 2011.

TC 7-100.3. Irregular Opposing Forces. 17 January 2014.

TC 7-100.4. *Hybrid Threat Force Structure Organizational Guide*. 4 June 2015.

OTHER PUBLICATIONS

Assessing and Evaluating Department of Defense Efforts to Inform, Influence, and Persuade: Desk Reference. Copyright © 2015. Christopher Paul, Jessica Yeats, Colin P. Clarke, & Miriam Matthews. RAND National Defense Research Institute. http://www.rand.org/content/dam/rand/pubs/research_reports/RR800/RR809z1/RAND_RR809z1.pdf

Assessing and Evaluating Department of Defense Efforts to Inform, Influence, and Persuade: Handbook for Practitioners. Copyright © 2015. Christopher Paul, Jessica Yeats, Colin P. Clarke, & Miriam Matthews. RAND National Defense Research Institute. http://comm.eval.org/HigherLogic/System/DownloadDocumentFile.ashx?DocumentFileKey=45b2d092-0c76-4a81-a13a-f1f0087c2dce

Assessing and Evaluating Department of Defense Efforts to Inform, Influence, and Persuade: An Annotated Reading List. Copyright © 2015. Christopher Paul, Jessica Yeats, Colin P. Clarke, & Miriam Matthews. RAND National Defense Research Institute. http://www.rand.org/content/dam/rand/pubs/research_reports/RR800/RR809z3/RAND_RR809z3.pdf

Dominating Duffer's Domain: Lessons for the 21st-Century Information Operations Practitioner (Report written for the Marine Corps Information Operations Center) Copyright © 2015. Christopher Paul and William Marcellino. RAND National Defense Research Institute.

PRESCRIBED FORMS

None

REFERENCED FORMS

Unless otherwise indicated, DA Forms are available on the Army Publishing Directorate (APD) web site: http://armypubs.army.mil.

DA Form 2028. *Recommended Changes to Publications and Blank Forms*.

Index

Entries are by paragraph number.

By order of the Secretary of the Army:

MARK A. MILLEY
General, United States Army
Chief of Staff

Official:

GERALD B. O'KEEFE
Administrative Assistant to the
Secretary of the Army
1634003

DISTRIBUTION:

Active Army, Army National Guard, and U.S. Army Reserve: To be distributed in accordance with the initial distribution number (IDN) 115425 requirements for FM 3-13.

Hand Signals

I Think I Saw Something

Did You Mean Me? (confirmation requested)

Looks Clear - No Need To Be Quie

Speak Up

I'm Having A Hard Time Seeing Very Far Without My Glasses

Aim for The Ass

I Can't Reach This Pocket (assistance requested)

I Have Been Hit (showing approximate size of hole)

Something's Wrong With My Gur (repeat gesture to add "..again!" t indicate frustration)

Printed in Great Britain
by Amazon